MANKIND MY CHURCH

MANKIND MY CHURCH

COLIN MORRIS

2369

Abingdon Press

Nashville   New York

MANKIND MY CHURCH

Copyright © 1971 by Colin Morris

ISBN 0-687-23137-X

Library of Congress Catalog Card Number: 78-185547

MANUFACTURED BY THE PARTHENON PRESS,
NASHVILLE, TENNESSEE, UNITED STATES OF AMERICA

For
Kenneth David Kaunda

PREFACE

These sermons make no pretensions to originality. Indeed, considering the sheer volume of sermons preached throughout Christian history, it could be argued that any truly original sermon would probably be grotesquely heretical. Anyway, unless he wants to found a new religion, it is not the preacher's job to be original. From time to time he may be tempted to believe that some pristine truth of God, which has lain dormant for twenty centuries, has taken up residence in his mind. But almost before the blinding flash of revelation has died away, he will be deflated to discover that some giant of the church, centuries before, has toyed with the same idea before effectively demolishing it.

So I acknowledge with gratitude those seminal minds as well as workaday preachers who have provided the raw material of my preaching. In particular, I wish to make reparation for those whose theological ideas I have appropriated and whose source I can no longer trace or remember. The continuing power of preaching has been demonstrated both by the impact they made upon me at the time and the ease with which they have become part of my thoughtways.

Colin Morris
Wesley's Chapel, London

ACKNOWLEDGMENTS

The following sources I can acknowledge specifically:

The two sermons on "The Rule of God over the World of Nations" are based on an address I gave to the 1966 World Methodist Conference. To prepare it, I put myself to school with Reinhold Niebuhr, whom I have found to be an unrivaled help in making theological sense of the freedom struggle in Zambia which has occupied me for the past decade. "Sacrifice or Waste?" owes both ideas and illustrations to Kenneth Slack's *Is Sacrifice Outmoded?* (S.C.M. Press, 1966). Paul Tillich was the source of ideas in both "The Realm of a Deathless 'Yes'" and "Saved by Cosmic Man." In the deep recesses of my mind, I vaguely recall an American preacher, whom regretfully I cannot name, using the text on which "Before Winter" is based, and I wouldn't be surprised if some of the ideas were his too.

My use of all these sources has been idiosyncratic, and in acknowledging my debt to these theologians and preachers I must also absolve them from any responsibility for the strange twists to which I have subjected their ideas.

CONTENTS

1. *The Devil in the Church* 11

2   *The Hiddenness of God* 22

3. *Prisoners of Hope* 31

4. *Prophet or Loss?* 42

5. *Before Winter* 52

6. *The Realm of a Deathless Yes* 59

7. *Mankind My Church* 71

8. *Sacrifice or Waste?* 84

9. *Holy Unemployable?* 93

10. *Saved by Cosmic Man* 105

11. *The Tensions of Ministry* 116

12. *The Rule of God over the World of Nations: 1* ..132

13. *The Rule of God over the World of Nations: 2* ..143

CHAPTER 1

The Devil in the Church[1]

I was told in theological college (not, I hasten to interject, by my tutors but by fellow students returning battered from their first pastorate) that the Devil enters the church through the choir. And I'm sure there are laymen quite convinced that the Devil comes into the church through the door of the minister's vestry.

Behind the parody is a hard truth. In that "unseen warfare" about which Paul talks, there are times when the church has undoubtedly served as the Devil's fifth column in the ranks of those who fight for God. You take the point without my reciting a catalog of those moments of black betrayal in the church's history and contemporary life.

I make no apology for calling evil by that old-fashioned, personal name, the Devil. It is a good way of keeping us alert to the fact that there is about the operation of evil the subtlety of a malevolent personality rather than the crudity of a blind, irrational force.

Possibly the Devil's most successful ploy is to get us to oversimplify this problem. In particular, there are what might be called the two wilderness temptations of the church. In the first, the Devil tries to assure us that the church is the one community to which he has no access, thus destroying our witness through complacency and egotism. In the second, we are tempted to write off the church as totally demonic, with the result that we are paralyzed and in despair.

A moment's reflection gives the lie to both.

[1] Broadcast in B.B.C. Lenten Series "Who Shall Deliver Us?"

How can the church be invulnerable to evil? We are the church. Are we invulnerable? The church is not a special order of creation but simply the company of those who follow Jesus. It is made of the same stuff as the world. In fact, it *is* the world shot through with the reconciling power of God. And if the church had been given divine exemption from sin, it would be useless as a testimony to what is humanly possible under God. It could no more say to the world "Look to us! Do it our way!" than an athlete could invite a man with two broken legs to do the high jump. Only if the church faces the same handicaps as the world can it serve as a pacemaker.

And what about that sinister figure—anti-Christ—about whom Jesus warns us in the Gospels? He suggests that when things really come to the boil, evil appears in a guise so similar to goodness that it is hard to tell them apart. Dismiss, if you will, anti-Christ as prescientific mythology. But it rings true, this picture of evil whose subtlety lies in getting us to do the right thing, almost; and to say the right thing, almost. What Jesus seems to be saying is that the Devil is more likely to appear carrying a hymn book than a fork; more likely to take up his abode on the bench of bishops or in the second pew from the front than in haunts of vice and degradation.

If anti-Christ apes Christ so successfully, then we in the church who live by faith and not by sight are bound, from time to time, to go haring off after anti-Christ, convinced that we are following Jesus.

The breathtaking claims we make assure us of the Devil's closest attention. If we live up to them, we shall become the Devil's number-one target; and if we don't, he has already got a foothold through our hypocrisy and pride.

Then there is that second wilderness temptation of the church. "I hate the church," writes an American theologian. "It is Judas, standing squarely in the way of the will of God."

Surveying sorrowfully our poor showing, we can sympathize with those who dismiss the church as totally demonic. But it can't be true. And that is not a pious hope but a matter of common sense. We can deny the church any more status than the rest of society, but we can hardly deny it less. Only if the whole world is totally demonic can the church be. And this is a rejection of the doctrine of creation, which asserts that nothing and no one, not even the Devil, is totally demonic. Nothing within history can ever be *completely* resistant to God's will. If there were such a being or community or area of society, then it would be outside God's control, and there could be no point of contact between it and the rest of creation. The question "Who shall deliver us?" would then be purely academic.

It is the besetting sin of the radical Christian (and I count myself one of them) that he is often concerned to offer redemption to a world that doesn't want it and deny it to the church, which with all its faults, is praying for it.

This question of the relationship of the church to evil is all very confusing. But as in so many other things, Jesus goes straight to the heart of the matter in one of his parables—the parable of the wheat and the tares.

Wheat and weeds grow together in a field, nourished by the same sun, often indistinguishable and always inseparable until they are cut down at harvest time. So it is, says Jesus, with good and evil in this life. History is not a success story—a saga of the irresistible onward march of goodness and the inexorable pushing back of evil. History is a tragedy, which is not to say that it is sad but that it is the scene of an interplay between good and evil which reaches a tremendous climax "at harvest time." Far from evil being systematically eradicated as time wears on, even in the eleventh hour, when the final vindication of goodness is at hand, anti-Christ—the ultimate embodiment of evil, to use Jesus' image—makes a last bid to frustrate God's purposes.

13

In the meantime, the very best actions of which men are capable, twisted by a bent world, let loose a flood of consequences both good and bad. This is not a cheerful view of history, but it is a realistic one. We don't have to look far for examples of this interplay of good and evil in the events of our own time.

Man unlocks the energy of the atom. That is good—one more evidence of his God-given dominion over the world of nature. But the consequences of this wholesome discovery are mixed. There are creative results such as the cobalt bomb which can destroy cancer cells, and evil ones such as the hydrogen bomb which threatens the future of mankind. But the outward ripple of this discovery does not stop even there. This wicked thing, the hydrogen bomb, has, paradoxically, the good effects of forcing an uneasy peace upon the world because the alternative is unthinkable. In the words of Winston Churchill, "Peace has become the sturdy child of Terror."

Or consider one lesson of the Nigerian conflict. The plight of starving Biafrans seared the conscience of the world, so that supplies of food and drugs poured in—a humanitarian action if ever there was one. This good deed had both the good effect of saving the lives of the hungry and sick, but also the evil one of prolonging the war. This is not an argument for doing nothing in such tragic situations, but it is a warning against imagining that simple goodness will always have purely beneficial effects in complex issues.

This is life; not a neat, tidy, morally transparent business, but a murky ambiguous one in which there is interwoven triumph and tragedy, beauty and terror, majesty and madness, fire and love. This is the kind of world within which the church is set, so need we be surprised that the servant of the highest becomes from time to time the slave of the ignoble; that the banner of God's army is besmirched with blood and the hands of God's servants leprous with sin?

14

This truth about the interweaving of good and evil in life is so complicated and terrifying that it is the besetting temptation of the church to retreat from the battlefield into a citadel of personal pietism—to scale down the problem and deal with the Devil in the church by the simple expedient of exorcising him from the heart of the individual Christian.

Now make no mistake about it, a gospel which does not offer personal redemption is no gospel. The human heart is the first outpost of God's rule in the world. Whatever may be the political and social implications of Jesus' teaching, he was first and foremost concerned with the quality of the personal life of the believer. So it is no small part of the task of exorcising the Devil from the church that individual Christians should be brought face to face with the gospel. But we cannot leave matters there.

Jesus came to establish a kingdom, not merely to gather together a fellowship of the redeemed. His target was the whole of creation and not just the tiny part of it upon which we have raised our cathedrals and tin tabernacles. The exorcism of the Devil from the church, or to use the jargon of our day, the church's renewal, is not an operation which takes place in isolation from, or as a prelude to, the renewal of the world. The church is only renewed at the same time as, and to the same extent that, the whole earth is renewed. We cannot save ourselves and let the world go to the Devil. It's all or nothing, this salvation business.

Because Jesus has chosen to fashion his kingdom out of the ambiguous stuff of history, the church has no option but to plunge into the murky pond of life where the mud is thickest and the light dimmest. And we have to take the consequences. We cannot sidestep those pressure points where the only practical choice that faces men is not between the transparently good and the obviously evil, but between the bad and the worse. And this means laying the church's reputation on the line and risking being compromised in the

15

firm belief that it is better for the church to be sincerely wrong through taking positive action than immaculately right but totally irrelevant through doing nothing.

It was the American poet Archibald MacLeish who said that there are only two kinds of people in this world, the pure and the responsible. In that division the church stands always amongst the responsible rather than the pure, the engaged rather than the detached, amongst the red-bloodedly reckless rather than the anemically dignified. And this, because we follow Jesus who plunged into a Jordan soiled by a thousand bodies, lived amongst publicans and sinners, died alongside criminals, and rose again out of a cemetery of decaying corpses.

Before we are finished with this human drama, the Devil's hold upon us is likely to be stronger rather than weaker. Far from fastidiously lifting our skirts to avoid contamination by evil, we have got to walk where its miasma is most poisonous and its power most terrifying, believing with Paul that it is precisely where sin abounds that grace more abounds; that the kingdom of God is not for the good but for the desperate.

But what hope have we that we shall not be left to stew in our own juice if we plunge into the cauldron; that we shan't be dragged down by the gravitational pull of evil within history; that the Devil's grip upon the church will not throttle the life out of her? How, and by whom, shall we be delivered?

Go back to that parable of Jesus and notice two details we are apt to overlook in our morbid preoccupation with the spectacle of wheat thrusting upwards toward the light through a strangulating tangle of weeds. The first is concerned with God's original intention, the second with his final action.

"A man sowed good seed in his field, but during the night his enemy came and sowed weeds amongst the wheat." But the wheat was sown first. Note that: *the wheat was sown first*.

16

Life is not some wasteland on which seeds of wheat and weed, carried by the wind, drop fortuitously and take root. Life is God's field in which the wheat was sown first. Goodness is built into the structure of things from the very outset. Evil is the interloper with only squatter's rights. It is an alien force, pitting itself against the declared purpose of things.

From our worm's-eye view, the titanic struggle between good and evil may seem to be a battle of equals taking place on unclaimed ground. In fact, every evidence of evil is an act of cosmic defiance against the odds. We stand for the good, not in a morally neutral world—which would leave the issue in doubt, nor in an evil world—which spells despair: we stand for the good in a good world. According to the book of Deuteronomy, God puts before a discouraged people the choice which confronts them and throws in some good advice—"I have set before you this day life and good, death and evil: therefore choose life!" We *can* choose life in the confidence that the universe stands behind us when we do good and resists us when we do ill. "Why do you kick against the pricks?" God asks a Devil-driven Paul. There is a logic of inevitability about the drift of things, a point at which evil can no longer obscure the signs of the Maker's intention—the divine hallmark stamped upon all creation.

This affirmation that the universe is friendly, biased toward our good intentions, is no cause for facile optimism. Nor is it a reason for a complacent and nonchalant reliance upon God to vindicate his own plans. In the short run, evil can and does frustrate God's purposes, bringing down untold suffering upon his children. But it does make a difference to our morale to know that there is no dark, sinister force at the heart of the universe which laughs at our heroism, nor a gaping void into which the goodness and love we achieve is poured and lost for ever. Every tiny victory is an act of co-operation with the purposes of creation, a brick with our

17

name upon it in the final edifice, and so has a dignity and significance out of all proportion to its apparent result.

So however strong the Devil's grip upon the church, God's grip must be stronger for the same reason that an owner has greater claim upon his property than a temporary tenant. In our domestic struggle against evil we dare to hope for victory not because of our virtue, ability, or strength, but because it is unthinkable that God will let go of that which he has called into being. This is not a pious hope but the testimony of the church's history. Our story has not been one of a triumphal progression from glory to glory but a paradoxical counterpoint of sudden ends and strange new beginnings, of decay and restoration, of death and resurrection, of humiliation and exaltation. This is because the wheat *was* sown first and will fight its way upwards toward the light.

Finally, there is Jesus' assertion in the parable that there *will* be a harvest. Wheat and weeds are not left to rot in the field. It is their destiny to be gathered and separated. This must mean that history will neither drag on nor fizzle out. The conflict between good and evil is not a war without end. There is to be a grand finale when the tangled threads of the plot are unsnarled; when good and evil are truly seen for what they are and dealt with accordingly. Just as neither the wheat nor the weeds can precipitate this harvest nor organize it, but depend upon an outside agent to effect it, so the meaning of history must lie beyond itself—the harvest is not something which happens *in* history, but something that happens *to* history.

The popular but inaccurate description of the event through which good is finally vindicated and evil abolished is the second coming of our Lord. It is inaccurate because the Bible never refers to it in this way, and it tends to suggest that in the meantime Jesus is somewhere else rather than at work in the here and now. Nevertheless, the truth which is distorted by such bad terminology is a central theme of the gospel, and indeed, for me at least, the gospel does not make sense without it. It is a pity that the idea of the second coming has been overladen with such bizarre imagery that the greater part of the church has virtually abandoned it to the more exotic sects.

It is also a pity that in our obsession for tidings we have divided up Christian doctrine into a series of manageable and separate propositions. So we have come to think of the resurrection of our Lord and his decisive action to wind up history as distinct events. In fact, they belong together as cause and effect. What we call the second coming is not so much an extraterrestrial arrival as a subterranean upheaval— not someone dropping out of the sky but bursting out of a tomb; this time not once in a garden long ago but all over the place. It occurs when the consequences of Jesus' resurrection work themselves through at sufficient points within history for its texture to be changed. Not an easy concept to grasp, but Jesus gave us the clue in his image of the leaven. At first, the addition of the leaven to the lump seems to make no difference. There is nothing to be seen or heard. Then suddenly as a result of the leaven's secret operation, the whole lump is transformed.

So it is with the resurrection. Its implications are still working themselves through. It is not an event whose consequences have been dissipated by the passing of time, but a secret surge of new life into history which gains momentum all the while. On the surface nothing seems to change. Things go on much as they ever did. But at some point—"and no man knows the time," warned Jesus—that power will change the character of history so that what was obscure will be clarified and everything worthwhile which seemed to have been lost will be restored. God will be vindicated and evil banished. And what some men have suspected and others have feared and most have ignored will be overwhelmingly apparent—that Jesus has done this thing. He will have

19

"appeared" and in the words of Paul, "all life will be alive with his life."

In the meantime, he is not remote in heaven, preening himself to make a triumphal final intervention, but is secretly at work, stealing into human situations like a thief in the night, to use another biblical image, and transforming them wherever he can find men to do, for whatever motives, the things he did in the days of his flesh.

So whenever the church lives "by the power of his resurrection"—and it cannot make good its breathtaking claims on the basis of any other power—it is testifying to the truth that the end is already here—one bit of creation has been transformed.

Who shall deliver us? Jesus, by the power of his resurrection, who else? The evil which could not hold him down in death cannot wreak its creeping death upon us his church either, provided it is "alive with his life."

Yet the Devil, who could not prevent the decisive victory in Gethsemane, still tries to achieve minor ones in Wigan or Birmingham or wherever by tempting us to deny that we are the stuff of which Easter victories are made. We conclude gloomily that Easter was once and for all—a special dispensation from death's clay finger for a unique being. But Easter was no victory for him unless it is a victory for you; unless the power which raised Jesus has universal availability—for you, for your little patch, and for his church.

To be alive with his life is not to rate any exemption from the Devil's attention any more than Jesus was exempt; it is an assurance that even when we are up to our necks in the torrent, we won't go under. We won't go under because beneath our feet is the firm foundation of a bit of God's new creation which cannot be eroded away by the dark and sinister elements in this life.

But don't let's delude ourselves about the basis of Christian hope. All our fidelity and service and witness cannot speed up by one moment that decisive event when evil is banished and the texture of history is changed into the material of a new heaven and a new earth. The initiative remains absolutely God's, and he shares it with no one. But we are entitled to a share in determining the form of that new creation. The Christian mission is a cooperative venture in which God allows full scope for human creativity.

So let's get on with it.

CHAPTER 2

The Hiddenness of God

This is a theme which is at once impossibly difficult and yet urgently topical. "Truly," says Isaiah, "Thou art a God that hidest thyself" and many people in our day would probably add, ". . . and you've made such a good job of it that we haven't the foggiest idea where to start looking for you!"

Let's be quite clear at the outset about the true nature of the problem. By God's "absence," I do not mean those times when because of our doubt or faithlessness, we have no sense of his presence. That problem, though difficult to cope with, is at least easy to understand. But what about a more serious possibility—that God chooses to absent himself from the world not because of our failure but by an act of his will? Suppose there are times, not when we have no sense of his presence, but when he really is not there?

Some Christians would say that this just isn't possible. God must always be *there*; the fault is in us for losing contact with him. Yet the basis of traditional Christian theology is the affirmation that at a certain point in time God appeared in history. If he can appear in this way, why cannot he also choose to disappear? We place intolerable limits upon God's freedom when we assume that he must always be ready to jump at our commands and appear on stage the moment we choose to raise the curtain.

What about the evidence of the Bible? From one angle, certainly, the Bible is the record of God's progressive revelation of himself. But there is another, darker theme running through it, of God's inexplicable disappearances, leaving men to stew in their own juice.

"Verily," says Isaiah, "Thou art a God that hidest thyself," or Job lamenting, "O, that I knew where I might find him!" or the psalmist crying, "My God, my God, why hast thou forsaken me?" or the Israelites at the time of Jehosophat, bemoaning the lack of prophets to show them where God was, or that terrible verse at the beginning of the letter to the Romans where Paul refers to one sorry lot of people and adds, "therefore, God gave them up." And there is also a tiny but significant detail in one of the parables of Jesus—"A man planted a vineyard, let it to tenants *and then went abroad.*"

Add to this biblical evidence the testimony of those modern theologians who state flatly that God is dead. The phrase may be semantic nonsense but it must speak of an experience which is real to them. Or take a playwright like Tennessee Williams, who puts into the mouth of one of the characters in *Sweet Bird of Youth* this phrase—"The speechlessness of God is a long, long terrible thing!" Add to all this the thousands of ordinary people who from the depths of their misery or the crest of their prosperity sneer, "Where is your God?" and you get some idea of the dimension of the problem.

Now we pulpiteers, confronted with this jarring evidence, are sometimes tempted to take the easy way out. We claim that God is *there* all right; it's just that men are looking for him in the wrong places. We seize upon the contrast between the form of Jewish messianic expectations and their fulfillment in Jesus—you know; they were looking for a king in royal panoply and did not notice the one who appeared in workman's overalls. Or we find the theme of the play *Waiting for Godot* particularly useful in making our point. Two tramps hang around, awaiting a critical event—the arrival of Godot. Instead, along comes Pozzo, leading his tame slave Lucky on a leash. The tramps become irritated at the antics of Pozzo. They can't be bothered with that sort of nonsense: they are waiting for Godot. But the playwright gives us to understand that Godot is *in* the nonsense.

23

It is very neat, this preacher's ploy. But it won't do, because it denies the actual experience of men within history. In slightly over one hundred years, we have moved from "All things bright and beautiful"—with its message that even a tiny child can see a world alive with God—to a situation where for the majority of people the universe echoes hollowly with God's absence.

No, this is a problem we have to face head on, in a series of tough propositions.

THE PURPOSE OF CREATION IS NOT TO REVEAL GOD BUT TO HIDE HIM

A moment's reflection shows that this must be so. Make the old-fashioned and daring assumption that God exists at all, then whatever else he may be, he must be ultimate reality. And it is the purpose of creation to protect us from the impact of a reality so intense that we would be destroyed by it. Demonsthenes once wrote, "If you cannot bear the candle, how will you face the sun?"

And we cannot bear the candle. Our human systems operate with the finest of tolerances. If our temperatures rise or fall by a mere ten degrees, we die. Both too much noise and too much silence will drive us mad. Too much pressure and we explode; too little, and we collapse like pricked balloons. We can only bear a tiny bit of reality. Indeed, from one angle, technology can be seen as a series of devices to cushion us from the impact of too much reality —air-conditioning to keep out the heat, central heating to protect us from the cold, buildings to shield us from the elements.

And it is not just from too much *physical* reality that we have got to be protected. We can take just so much love, so much truth, so much joy—the plenitude of experience would blow every fuse in our nervous systems. How, then, could we cope with God—ultimate reality—if his intolerable impact

24

were not veiled by creation? "No man," said God to Moses, "can see me face to face and live."

A West African creation myth puts the point beautifully. In the beginning God existed, and so did men. But God was pure God, naked God, and men were afraid to go near him. So God covered himself with the mantle of creation—rivers in which men could fish, forests in which they could hunt, soil which they could cultivate. Thus men lost their fear of approaching God—and God, so the story quaintly ends, was as happy as a dog with fleas.

Life within history is only possible at all because of God's hiddenness. For God's presence embodies his judgment; his unequivocal presence must confront men with a sort of premature judgment which would render creation pointless and bring down the curtain on the drama of mankind before it had truly begun. You see this in the Old Testament when God says to Moses, "You go up to the Promised Land, but I am not coming with you, lest I consume you on the way because of your sinfulness!" That epic trek through the wilderness could never have been completed in the unequivocal presence of God.

There is such a thing as overwhelming presence paralyzing action. Tell an amateur pianist about to give a recital that Sviatoslav Richter is in the audience, and you see what I mean. Without doubt, Richter would be generous in his judgment and praise, but that isn't likely to be much consolation to the hapless amateur about to strike the first note with fingers that have suddenly become as mobile as a bunch of bananas. To put it in human terms, our struggle to fulfill ourselves depends upon God's tactful withdrawal whilst we make our inevitable mistakes, otherwise we should be tempted to throw in the towel and relegate ourselves to the lower orders of creation—those beings who fulfill themselves involuntarily merely by existing because they have been denied the freedom to do anything else.

It is being widely claimed that any effective evangelism in our day depends upon a rediscovery of natural theology—that knowledge of God which is to be gathered together from the evidence of God's presence within creation by the use of our reason. I personally believe that we would speak more to the mood of our time if we investigated the ways in which God is hidden from us by creation and the reasons why.

But to take the argument on a further stage, here is an even more difficult proposition.

THERE ARE TIMES WHEN GOD'S ABSENCE IS THE FORM OF HIS PRESENCE

The more I try to bend my mind around this problem, the easier it is to understand why the Jews would never utter the name of God, and why there was nothing—no idol or likeness of him—in the holy of holies behind the curtain of the great temple. In what was *not* uttered there was eloquent testimony, and in nothingness there *was* brooding presence.

It is both man's greatest achievement and besetting sin that he has an irresistible urge to reduce all truth and experience to manageable proportions—to cut it down to *his* size. Given half a chance, we would do the same to God—try to reduce him to manageable proportions. And we would be so taken up with disputes about the degree to which our guesses about him measured up to his actual reality that our attention would be distracted from the world which is the sphere of our reasonable service. But paradoxically, in his absence is a form of presence which we cannot inspect, measure, label, and then consign to a museum along with all the other concrete evidences of our crusade for truth.

Take a more homely illustration of this strange truth. My father was a powerful personality who effortlessly and benevolently dominated our entire household. He died whilst I was away in Africa, and I returned to my family home with some foreboding to find, as I expected, his favorite chair empty,

26

his pipe, long unlit, on the mantelshelf. But I found something else too; that even in his absence, he still dominated the room in which he was forced to spend his last days. His absence was a special form of his presence—special because it was multi-dimensional. Had I met him face to face on walking into that room, I would have been conscious only of how he was at that moment, but the form of presence his absence created encompassed a whole range of memories that spanned my lifetime. In one sense, his absence was a more comprehensive form of his presence at that moment than any face-to-face encounter.

In much the same way, absence is one essential form of the presence of a *God of history*. For faith must encompass not only what God is, but also what he has ever been from the beginning—"I am the God who brought you out of the land of Egypt," he keeps on reminding the Jews whenever they get off track and forget the reason for their existence as a people. God's certain presence could so overawe and preoccupy us that our sense of historical responsibility could give way to mystical contemplation:

> Transported by the view I'm lost
> In wonder, love and praise.

Yes; but not yet, for as Robert Frost put it:

> I have promises to keep
> And miles to go before I sleep.

Our generation shows an intense preoccupation with God's absence. At a time when we are assured that Christianity is on the way out, serious journals and newspapers devote acres of space to God-talk. Those theologians who are so inclined are not content to pronounce God dead and then go about their earthly business. They stand, mesmerized, gazing into his grave. Philosophers write five-hundred-page books proving the impossibility of belief in God. Whoever heard of anyone writing a five-hundred-page book proving the impossibility of belief in Santa Claus or fairies? This God-shaped blank at

27

the heart of our society is emitting some kind of signal that keeps the minds of thoughtful men in turmoil. If it is any part of God's purpose to get men to think and talk about him, this strategic withdrawal has been a brilliant success.

Many Christians would claim that there is one great exception to this rule that God's absence is the form of his presence—Jesus. Was not God fully revealed in him? I think not. Though it would be absurd to instance Jesus as evidence of God's *absence* from men, it seems to me that Jesus was the one in whom God was most completely *hidden*—which is one reason why the New Testament goes to such lengths to avoid any simple identification of God with Jesus.

Those who saw Jesus looked upon a man; it was a man's voice they heard and a man's actions they observed. And they were judged by their reaction to a man. Had they looked at Jesus and seen God in his own light, unmistakably *there*, then the whole point of the incarnation would have been lost. To be looking for God, to have seen him, and then not to have followed would have been madness; unbelief would shade into simple disobedience, and faith would cease to be important or even necessary.

Jesus himself had to wrestle with this sense of the hiddenness of God: why else did he echo on the cross the words of the psalmist, "My God, my God, why hast thou forsaken me?" Why else did he point men away from himself and toward God with his repeated warning, "Tell no man!"? And why did he insist upon keeping those who wished to soar away to heaven firmly earthed in the world of men?

No one can quarrel with those who throughout Christian history have felt that Jesus' sense of unity with the source of all being was so complete that he warrants the adjective "divine." But Jesus never claimed divinity for himself. Indeed, he did not ask that men should pray to him, sing about him, or even worship him. He made upon them one strictly human demand: Follow me.

28

If it be charged that to claim Jesus was "only a man" is to perpetrate the great humanist heresy, then I must plead guilty. I do not see how anyone who was fully a man could be "more than a man," or even why he need be "more than a man" to do the work God laid upon him. Since I am agnostic about the objective existence of supernatural beings called angels, it must follow that within the rules of creation which God himself made, he has no higher forms of being than man through whom to work. I can follow Teilhard de Chardin in his depiction of Jesus as the crown of the evolutionary process —cosmic man, the Christ of the Universe. Or I can change the scale and say that Jesus was truly man whilst the rest of us are still subhuman, not fully developed. But my faith depends upon accepting that God was totally hidden in the *man* Jesus.

This suggestion that God's absence is the form of his presence puts human doubt and despair in a new light. Our sense of outrage when we reach the raw edge of life and find that God is not there and feel *he ought to be* is a cry of faith; our mourning for a lost God sounds a *Te Deum*. And our inability to fill that God-shaped blank with idols sketches the true dimensions of God more clearly than all the positive descriptions of him in the creeds.

And this affirmation of God's absence also has a practical outworking of great importance. It provides the cutting edge of our social action. If one may so term it, the fact that God gets out of the way—steps out of the picture—enables us to invest our fellowmen with ultimate significance, even though we know that in the strictly theological sense they cannot have ultimate significance, since that value belongs to God alone. I can *see* God, for example, in the outcast, the prisoner, and afflicted, only because I can *see* him nowhere else. Hence, to use ungodly language, I can with God's connivance lavish upon my fellowmen a quality of concern and service which are his by right. I am a humanist by divine permission.

What, then, is the point of God hiding himself?

29

IT IS OUR FREEDOM AND MATURITY WHICH ARE AT STAKE

You ask: why does God hide himself? Why does a parent step back from an infant taking his first faltering steps? Why does a wise boss avoid constantly looking over the shoulder of a worker? So that we can probe the very limits of what is humanly possible. So that every time we stumble, we do not reach out for a divine crutch; so that when things get tight, we do not throw up our hands and wallow in irresponsible pietism.

God's presence is the time of human realization; his absence puts us still in the time of human potentiality. Because we are men, all shortcuts to truth are barred to us—even divine ones. For what is the point of creating men capable of dreams and giving them nothing to dream about? Why make them capable of achievement and leave nothing unachieved? Say to man that there are no more symphonies to write, no more mountains to climb, no more refinements of the human spirit to attain, and a light will go out in his mind. To be a man is to reach for things beyond my grasp, or manhood is not worth having.

So God's hiddenness is not a confession that the world has gotten out of his hands. It is a vote of confidence in you—he has placed it in your hands. Faith is a two-way business. God's faith in us is at least as important as our faith in him. And often that will be the only faith operative in our lives. When we lose our faith in him, we can survive on the realization that he has not lost faith in us. His hiddenness is a supreme demonstration of his faith in us; an affirmation that he has left the world in good hands. We know that more often than not this confidence is misplaced. It is just not true that this world is in good hands when it is placed in our hands, but we have been given a powerful incentive to make it true.

This is the nub of the issue. The world belongs to God and will be what we make it.

CHAPTER 3

Prisoners of Hope[1]

"To your stronghold, you prisoners of hope."
Zechariah 9:12.

I was sitting in Lusaka International Airport the other day, reflecting somewhat gloomily about the present state of Africa—undeclared war in Arab Africa, postwar wound-licking in Nigeria, civil and religious strife in Chad and the Sudan, and now an iron shutter crashing down in Rhodesia to cut off white Africa from the rest of the continent. Things looked so unpromising; yet at that moment there came unbidden into my mind this phrase from Zechariah—prisoners of hope. So my text for this sermon chose itself.

There can now be little doubt that the confrontation between black and white Africa has assumed the character of a Greek tragedy in which resolution only emerges from the far side of cataclysm. And in this tragedy, the main protagonists seem so committed to acting out a ritual destiny that it would not be inappropriate to call them "prisoners."

PRISONERS OF DESPAIR

The white minority governments of southern Africa and their supporters are prisoners of despair but not of pessimism. There is a buoyancy, a cock-sureness in their ability to buck history that is quite breathtaking. All the same, they *are* prisoners of despair.

When you are compelled to weave barbed wire around yourself as a protection against your fellow citizens, your

[1] Preached at Great St. Mary's, Cambridge, the week Rhodesia was declared a republic.

31

security is a form of imprisonment—you can only shut others out at the price of shutting yourself in.

When you are committed to a doctrine of history so cock-eyed that in comparison *Alice in Wonderland* reads as somberly as Bradshaw's *Railway Guide.* . . .

When highly intelligent people running a technologically advanced society, the moment they lift their noses out of their slide rules, revert to a philosophy of life which resounds to the rattle of ox-wagon wheels and the roar of Zulu hordes—a philosophy shored up by phony anthropology, mendacious statistics, and a crude mysticism of blood—to believe *that lot,* you have to do such violence to your intellect and integrity that despair seems too mild a word.

When you have such a chronic distrust of your fellow citizens of a different color that you dare not place yourself at their mercy; when you have so little confidence in the justice of your past dealings with them that you live in terror that one day you may be on the receiving end of the treatment you have handed out to them for centuries—then you are prisoners of despair.

When you dare not dance to the brave music being made in other parts of Africa (and in spite of Nigeria, there *is* brave, brave music being made in Africa); when you cannot give due credit to the tremendous achievements of the new nations of Africa but must exult in their setbacks, jeer at their triumphs, and rejoice in their agonies or else give the lie to the philosophy of black depravity upon which you have staked your existence—then brave, buoyant, and tough as you may be, you are trapped in a prison of despair.

PRISONERS OF OPTIMISM

In the drama of southern Africa, these are represented by the British government and her Western allies. The convolutions of recent British policy toward Africa are so opaque to the light of reason that the ordinary man must conclude they are

motivated by a dark Machiavellian subtlety which masquer-
ades with brilliant success as plain stupidity.

In particular, in its handling of the crisis caused by Rhodesia's Unilateral Declaration of Independence, the British
government has fallen victim to what might be called the
Houdini Syndrome; you know—"Tie us in a thousand chains
and throw us over Niagara Falls and in a trice we shall be
free!"—inviting mounting complications in order to demonstrate virtuosity in overcoming them. Optimism, pathetic optimism! "There'll be no U.D.I." "All right there has been
U.D.I. but it will all be over in a fortnight." "Well, all right,
they've survived the first year but our sanctions will get them
down sooner or later." And so every creak in Salisbury is
heralded in Whitehall as the first stone in a landslide which
will sweep away the Smith regime.

The optimism of our government is compounded of
unconscionable pride and utter unrealism. Their lack of
understanding of white settler psychology is limitless. Did
they seriously believe that the Smith government would
accept the *Tiger* and *Fearless* proposals and obligingly
commit political suicide? Would the Labor government
agree to constituency boundary changes which must produce
a Tory majority till the end of time? Yet they expect Mr.
Smith to implement a constitution whose ultimate result
must be to rob him and his supporters of political power forever and are hurt and disappointed when he refuses!
Optimism! Pathetic optimism!

These prisoners of optimism are hardheaded realists
about their own political prospects but expect others to be
hopeless idealists about theirs. And in the same category I
suppose we must count groups like the M.C.C. who think
that the South African government arranges its affairs
according to the laws of cricket, and that if you give the
Springboks a rattling good time at Lord's, they will dash off
back to Pretoria, advocating a change to the good old British

33

way of life—forgetting that South Africans turned their backs on the good old British way of life sixty years ago so that they would never have to rub shoulders with their colored brethren in cricket pavilions.

Indeed, in the present state of race relations in Britain, there is grave danger that the Springboks might take back with them quite the wrong message, and having observed the sorry spectacle of Kenyan Asians waving British passports as they are propelled like yoyos back and forth through the upper air, one might conclude that there's something to be said after all for honest-to-god *apartheid*.

The reason why both prisoners of despair and of optimism cannot make an adequate response to the situation in southern Africa is that they ignore two theological dimensions of all political problems.

1. *The radical nature of sin.*

When I left theological college, I did not pay much attention to all this Christian talk about sin, but after fifteen years of involvement in African politics, I am convinced that sin is a reality we ignore at our peril. Nations, racial groups, and political parties do not repent by a simple rational process of analyzing their past errors. There is a deep and all-pervasive corruption of the will at work within the body politic; and the prisoners of optimism in particular compound the old Marxist error of assuming that history itself is redemptive and that if it goes off course, it is self-correcting on the basis of some moral or political or economic gyroscope built into it. They ignore the warning of our Lord in the parable of the wheat and the tares that history is morally ambiguous—every extension of good becoming the springboard for new possibilities of evil.

2. *The grace of God.*

There is in operation in the political field a creative factor which does not spring naturally out of man's makeup or from his economic arrangements and political programs—a factor that I can only describe as the operation of the grace of God. It unsnarls logjams, spans unbridgeable gulfs, and resolves apparent deadlocks. I have seen this happen too often in concrete political situations ever to believe that talk about the grace of God is pious cant. It operates through men of affairs who make surprising renunciations and unpredictable sacrifices; who have unaccountable changes of mind and of heart, and as a consequence the stalemate of eyeball-to-eyeball diplomacy is broken, and mankind gets on the move again.

PRISONERS OF HOPE

Prisoners of hope, who are the third group of protagonists in the southern African drama, take due account of both these theological dimensions, though they may not dress them up in such fancy terminology. By so doing, they are preserved from the fundamental heresy of liberal politics—which is the belief that any international problem is soluble at a given point in time, provided we put more elbow grease, more dedication, and more ingenuity into its resolution. In fact, there are certain international problems which at any moment in history are strictly insoluble. I believe the problem of achieving justice for all the peoples of southern Africa is, at the present time, totally intractable, and, paradoxically, the possibility of hope depends upon coming to terms with this hard fact.

The prisoner of hope can live with an intractable problem without lying down under it and cursing a capricious fate that it is beyond his present capacity to resolve. He knows that there are certain times which are the days of small things, just as there are others which are days of grand strategies. And in the day of small things, it is often by very tiny hinges that great weights are moved.

Africa is rich in prisoners of hope because she has often

had to live in the day of small things through lack of technical resources and scientific sophistication, because of the dead weight upon her of superior alien cultures. Yet she has also seen mountains moved, deserts blossom, and has lived out the miracles of nationhood and human survival against all odds. So there is no doubt that Africa will evolve a strategy of hope for dealing with this intractable problem at the southern tip of the continent, and those who wish to identify themselves with her struggle would do well to share it.

Let me briefly sketch out three of the possible dimensions of such a strategy of hope.

1. *The ability to live in the present as though the future were already here.*

In Christian theology hope is always linked with the *parousia,* and the scholars tell me that *parousia* means both what is present and what is coming. Now there is in African experience and thought forms a sort of profane or secular or at least overtly non-Christian manifestation of *parousia.* For example, those of you who have tried to learn a Bantu language will know that present and future tenses are often hopelessly jumbled up. This has carried over into African politics. The peoples of Africa have a capacity for living in the present as though the future were already here which we in the West have lost, I think, because materialism supplies us with a bewildering variety of artifacts which provide a kind of barrier against the future—the material ballast that prevents us from packing our bags and getting on the move. If in a rich world, however, your only wealth is hope, it is amazing the ease with which you can smash through the metaphysical barrier between present and future.

Let me give you three illustrations of this.

At this moment in Moçambique there are large tracts of this Portuguese territory controlled by the Africa freedom movement—Frelemo. Inside an area honeycombed by

Portuguese troops, they have set up their own administration, organized schools and hospitals, and even their own police force. Frelemo's hold upon the area is fragile and should they be caught, the price they will pay is a grievous one. But they steadfastly refuse to live in a depressing present and insist upon molding their life in conformity with the future.

There are whites in southern Africa who at great personal cost show a majestic contempt for *apartheid*. They will have nothing to do with the pass laws or the Group Areas Act; they are determined not to be cut off from their colored brethren. They are living out the future in the midst of a cruel present and are paying sorely for the privilege.

In 1960 a great man—Kenneth David Kaunda—now President of the Republic of Zambia, then a nationalist leader on the run, sat in my house and sketched on a piece of paper a structure of government for a nonexistent state to be called Zambia. He also put marks on a map where schools and hospitals were to be built. At this time, the peoples of Zambia were trapped in the Federation of Rhodesia and Nyasaland which seemed invincible in its power to hold up their constitutional advance. Those of us who sympathized with President Kaunda were beside ourselves with frustration: he, on the other hand, sat quietly administering on paper a nonexistent state. Cynics might have sneered that he was like a child playing with soldiers, but when I drive now through Zambia and pass those very schools which were once pencil marks on a map, I realize the extent to which the African people have been preserved from this corrosive pessimism which makes Westerners scale down their visions to the point of what is practically possible at a given moment.

All over Africa prisoners of hope are living out the future in the midst of an unpromising present, some of them at great cost. But they will change the texture of history.

2. *A willingness to operate the small hinges by which great weights move.*

Every night Rhodesian Africans slip back into their own country and engage Rhodesian forces in unequal combat. Their armament is derisory, their numbers are pathetic, their losses are terrifying. But they have made a decision which we liberals in the West, sympathetic to their plight, balk at. They have seen that there are certain situations where the only hinge that moves great weights is force. And insofar as Christians wish to identify themselves with freedom struggles in Africa, Asia, and Latin America, this is one nettle they will have to grasp. It may be a sad thing, but in the twentieth century violence is one of the most important mechanisms of social and political change—a strictly temporary but sometimes effective solution to the problem of justice. Violence, to put it in Dantean terms, may well not establish a Paradise, but it can destroy an Inferno.

This is not a palatable subject for Christians, and it is understandable why we do not wish to give houseroom to the possibility that it might be right to make, under certain conditions, a positive affirmation of the value of violence. Without doubt this is a theological issue in comparison with which every other theological issue of our day pales into insignificance. The only sizeable group of Christians at the present time who have evolved a theology of violence are pacifists. I admit the validity of their vocation and admire their witness to an ideal law of the kingdom, but I do not believe that they articulate the only Christian position on this issue. Christian nonpacifists have, on the whole, avoided articulating their position, overcome by distaste at what they may be required to do to their fellowmen. This is understandable; but it will not do.

There is urgent need for a resumption of the dialogue between Christian pacifists and nonpacifists in the light of two realities of our day—nuclear weapons and revolution as an instrument of justice—which have rendered the old arguments and counterarguments irrelevant. In particular, those Christians who believe that the use of force can be squared with the gospel have an obligation to formulate a theology of violence which will lay down the conditions under which its use is permissible.

Because force is sometimes the only hinge by which great weights can be moved, we have got to bring the issue out into the open. We are entitled to say that we will have none of it or that under certain conditions its use is justified, but we are not entitled to adopt a position of soggy neutrality and pretend that the widespread ferment of our day is not happening. If nonpacifists have an obligation to explore in detail the conditions in which the use of force is permissible, pacifists have also the duty of taking a long, hard look at oppressive regimes such as those of southern Africa and offering a viable political strategy for achieving justice without the use of violence.

3. *The necessity for bringing to bear the moral pressure of the whole of mankind upon any one part of it.*

When we have finished bemoaning the grip of tribalism upon Africa and of pointing up the lessons of the tragedies of the Congo and Nigeria, it is still true that the spirit of internationalism has taken a greater hold in Africa in two decades than in three hundred years of European history. When the seventh wealthiest country in Africa is prepared to enter into economic union with a number of poorer states, knowing that she will end up paying most of the bills whilst they get most of the benefits, talk of African internationalism is not just pious idealism.

In a number of ways, my stay in Africa has made it impossible for me to think in terms of any allegiance less embracing than all mankind. I can see no virtue in blind patriotism and no realism in ecclesiastical affiliations. I have come to believe that anything, however worthwhile it may seem in itself, which cuts me off from my fellow human beings is evil. And this is not a vague, visionary sentiment. We are living in a time when prisoners of hope in every nation under the sun have become conscious of a common history and common experience and are moving toward a common destiny. It is, for example, now almost universally accepted that in the nuclear age the whole world is the smallest possible unit of survival.

The United Nations Organization is open to every conceivable form of criticism, yet it is the great prophetic fact of our day—prophetic in the sense that it points beyond itself to a true world community, to a time when its present gossamer web of international obligation, which can be snapped with contemptuous ease, will have been superseded by a strong and durable structure of ethics and law. But we cannot fold our arms and wait for that day. Those who believe that mankind is truly one and that this is where their primary allegiance lies must think and behave as citizens of the world. Southern Africa does not float in a vacuum. It is joined to the rest of our world by a thousand filaments. The Rhodesian immigration authorities can keep out undesirable persons, but they cannot keep out undesirable ideas. The power and spirit of our age expressed in such ways as a growing abhorrence of all forms of discrimination cannot be resisted indefinitely by ideological barriers or *apartheid* laws or phony declarations of independence.

When I am asked what Christians in Europe and the United States, who have no access to the corridors of power, can do to help their brethren in southern Africa other than all the paraphernalia of boycott, sanction, and demonstration, which seems so laughably inadequate, I would say that such gestures form part of the moral pressure which the whole of mankind can bring to bear upon any one part of it. One world; one humanity; therefore, one battleline. Every blow, every pathetic blow struck for racial equality and human dignity in Wolverhampton or Cambridge reverberates in Salisbury or Pretoria; every erosion of justice in Westminster, Washington, Moscow, or Peking slams shut a prison cell door in southern Africa. In the day of small things, the efforts of small men achieve a significance which would be denied them in the day of grand strategies that demand men of heroic proportions to work the levers of power.

So count me among the prisoners of hope, not because I have any clear idea at this minute where the road to justice and equality in southern Africa lies: I haven't. But I refuse to believe that the forward advance of all mankind will be held up by any group of people who try to hold a part of it in thrall. I may believe that history is mysterious, but I don't believe it's meaningless. And I believe in hope not so much in terms of resolution as in terms of resurrection, through seeds growing secretly and leaven transforming whole lumps. And it's not a humanist vision I've been putting across. For me Christ holds the key to the door of the cell in which the prisoners of hope work and pray and struggle to make what could be must be.

CHAPTER 4

Prophet or Loss?

"Would that all the Lord's people were prophets!"
Numbers 11:29.

The supreme compliment the church can pay a man at the present moment is neither to wrap episcopal gaiters round his legs nor a doctoral hood round his neck, but to attach the magic adjective "prophetic" to his name. Then his books sell like hot cakes and he packs in the students like sardines. He's got the Word!—as the disc jockeys say.

There are men and women in the modern church who are worthy to be named in the same breath as those Hebrew wild men of the Old Testament. They see things steadily and see them whole whilst the rest of us thrash around treating the world like a cheap watch—to be subjected to inexpert investigation until all the pieces lie in front of us, defying our efforts to put them back together again.

But true prophets are in such short supply that possibly Paul was right in regarding the prophetic office as a form of specialism. "He called some to be apostles, some prophets, some evangelists, some pastors and teachers." However, rightly or wrongly, throughout its history the church does not appear to have taken Paul very seriously. A man called to the ordained ministry has been expected to have a crack at all the jobs Paul catalogs as well as some others he'd never heard of, such as wearing out the seat of one's soul at committee meetings and licking stamps and other biblical pursuits.

God knows what would happen if a modern candidate for the ministry took Paul really seriously and announced that he felt "called to be a prophet"! The examiners would smell his breath, probe his family background for unfortunate Pente-costal tendencies, and then award him ten black marks for cheek in presuming to class himself with Dietrich Bonhoeffer.

There is New Testament support, I think, for rejecting the idea of prophecy as a rare specialism. The wry wish of Moses, "Would that *all* the Lord's people were prophets!" was granted a long time later at Pentecost where "*all* present were filled with the Spirit and began to speak." From that time on, prophecy ceases to be the monopoly of a specialized elite within the church and becomes an essential dimension in the witness of every Christian.

But how do we do it? That is the problem—what does it mean to be prophetic in our own little patch? We are most likely to get at an answer to that question by pointing up the differences between true and false prophets—noting, in passing, that there is no shortage of false prophets in the modern church!

1. *False prophets look to the Bible for answers: true prophets allow it to pose the questions.*

The Bible has declined in authority because of our insis-tence upon treating it like a one-volume encyclopedia of universal salvation. Name your problem and the Bible pundits will fire off a string of texts which they claim offer an infallible solution to it.

But the Bible is not a time capsule buried two thousand years ago and pre-programmed by God to bellow forth at the touch of a button instant answers to any question which history may throw up. With breathtaking gall, we tap on the shoulder men wrestling with complex issues which baffle the best minds of our day and assure them that the answers they seek are to be found in the Sermon on the Mount or the Ten Commandments or wherever. I suspect the world is getting very tired of well-meaning Christians scurrying around applying Jesus like a sticking plaster to its running sores.

43

This slab of history with the roof off we call the Bible; this record of the totality of a people's life lived out in the presence of God doesn't offer solutions to any problems other than those which arose in the times about which its authors were writing—and a fair number of those answers proved to be wrong! What the Bible does is to pose inescapable questions which men of this or any age evade at their peril, and it is these questions which are the touchstone of its relevance and contemporaneity.

God to Adam: "Where art thou?"

Isaiah to his people: "Why will this nation perish for disobeying God?"

Jesus to a sick woman: "What do you want me to do for you?"

Jesus to every Christian: "Why call me Lord and ignore the things I command you?"

Paul and Barnabas to the people of Lystria: "Why do you put your trust in gods that cannot save?"

These formal questions, of which I've given you a few examples, together with the questions which are raised in your own minds by reading the Bible, are special questions because they demand not academic answers but personal responses. They are God's questions to men and are meant to issue in costly action rather than interesting discussion.

God's word is in the questions because he treats us as men, giving scope for human creativity in seeking the answers. He does not reduce us to mindless megaphones, passing on to our fellowmen messages broadcast from a transmitting station beyond the stars and put in written form by courtesy of the British and Foreign Bible Society.

Take, for example, a burning issue of our day, the question of violence as a solution to the problems of justice. If we go to the Bible, seeking some resolution of the grievous dilemmas rooted in the relationship between love and power, we end up pacifist versus nonpacifist, standing eyeball-to-eyeball, hitting each other over the head with contradictory texts—Matthew's Jesus saying that those who live by the sword will perish by it, against Luke's Jesus advising his disciples to go out and buy swords. If, however, we steep ourselves in the questions raised by the history of God's Israel and in the life and death of Jesus, it may be possible for both pacifist and nonpacifist to make creative responses to those questions without either one denying the light by which the other walks.

To put the matter baldly: the false prophet says that life raises questions to which the Bible supplies answers; the true prophet looks for creative responses in his own life and the life of his society to the questions which the Bible poses.

And if there is a dearth of true prophecy in the church, it is because we have treated the world for too long as a captive audience—to be lectured, preached at, exhorted, and damned. Because of our much speaking, we have not listened and so have not heard the variety of responses which the world is making to all sorts of questions, both important and trivial. It is from the answers which the world returns to the questions the Bible poses that the raw material of prophecy is fashioned.

2. *The false prophet is a moralist—he tells the world how things ought to be: the true prophet is a realist—he tells the world how things really are.*

It is interesting to conjecture why the Bible has never been censored. Why was it not cleaned up before publication like the parliamentary record in those countries where politicians are allowed to erase their more asinine remarks before the public get their hands upon it? There is a rigorous honesty about the Bible which takes one's breath away. It tells us the way it was, not the way we or anyone else would have liked it to have been. So the dark, blood-stained bits have been left in; the arrant paganism; the flirting with false gods; those bursts of hatred and malevolence that almost curl the edges of the paper.

The Bible tells it the way it is because the truth is redemptive. Before World War I, Woodrow Wilson said this: "The new radicalism [in politics] consists not in the things proposed but in the things disclosed." A better definition of prophecy it would be difficult to find. The prophet is not a moralist, proposing ideal programs of action; he is a realist, uncovering the truth about situations as they are.

This determination to tell it the way it is cannot be too highly prized in a society which is adept at self-delusion; which puts unpleasant things in fancy wrappings, and gives pretty names to ugly realities. We talk about aid when we mean fraud, development when we mean exploitation. We say in justification for the Vietnam war that we are making Asia safe for democracy when what we mean is fighting for the security of the West to the last drop of Asia's blood. Some people in Britain talk about sending colored immigrants back home because they will feel happier amongst their own kind, but what is really meant is that we are too scared, too lazy, or too superior to compete with them for jobs.

A whole new industry has grown up dedicated to providing those who can pay for the service with a "good" image, and these professional whitewash merchants are sufficiently skilled to project the Jesse Jameses of public life as though they were the Good Samaritan. There are advertising agencies who can doctor manure so that it tastes like caviar and smells of attar of roses and then convince the public that no home is complete without the delicacy.

Whenever men say one thing and mean another; wherever they try to oversimplify complex issues or make simple issues complex; wherever men are apt to delude themselves or seek to delude others, there is a crying need for prophets who will tell it as it is—get under the rationalization and verbiage and uncover the truth. Never mind about proposing fancy programs in terms of what ought to be in the best of all possible worlds. The prophetic task is to get at the truth in this world, believing that every testimony to the truth is a testimony to the one who is the Truth. For however pleasant or sordid, hard or easy, the truth of any situation may be, that truth, by its nature, is redemptive and creative; it both judges and heals.

We have got to tell it the way it is because we believe that God is not remote in the ultimate Why of things but close at hand in the immediate How of them. True prophets tell it the way it is, not in the upper reaches of the universe, but on the lower floors of the factory or municipal offices.

3. *False prophets offer men easy harmonies: true prophets confront them with hard choices.*

The besetting sin of most good men is inflexibility. Their very single-mindedness in pursuing worthwhile goals often frustrates their honest intentions by twisting their virtues into vices—spirituality shades into remoteness, integrity hardens into legalism, earnestness tends toward aggression, fervor escalates into fanaticism. By the same token, the too rigorous pursuit of the truth can lead men into error—an insight which caused Lord Acton to write: "When you perceive a truth, look for a balancing truth." In all but the simplest human situations, truth is more likely to emerge from the tension of opposing viewpoints than from a rigid statement of principle.

This insight about the complex nature of the truth is the ultimate justification for democracy as a political system. If government has hold of a truth, the opposition have the freedom to search for and state "the balancing truth," and so from the tension of these two viewpoints something like justice is likely to be achieved. That is the theory. But what happens when people have, in principle, freedom of choice, but there aren't different things to choose from?

47

It is a situation something like this which strikes me as the most dangerous feature of the current political system in Britain. There has been a move toward consensus politics, with the policies of government and opposition parties becoming almost indistinguishable, so that strong principles have dissolved in a mish-mash of dirty gray moderation. False prophets in our society applaud this development as proof that we are all pulling together or living in harmony. In fact, what it means is that those groups within society such as colored immigrants or students or National Front supporters, who *have* strong principles and are not prepared to swap them for the mass of quivering jelly which passes for a common mind, may decide that there is no place for them in the system and so begin to work for its overthrow.

The true prophet's role in such a time is to dispel the euphoria of false harmony and insist on showing society that there are still hard choices to be made and spelling out what those choices are. He will, of course, be accused of provocation and incitement, of disturbing the peace and spreading trouble. But didn't Jeremiah once warn that it is the ultimate betrayal of the prophetic office to cry "peace, peace, where there is no peace"?

True prophecy is the constant search for the balancing truth, the other point of view which is in danger of being ignored or shouted down. My book *Unyoung, Uncolored, Unpoor,* for all the wrath it brought down upon my head, was one such an attempt to state a balancing truth, to show the West that its virtues had, over the years, hardened into vices, and that it must face the real possibility of revolution if the blatant injustices it had perpetrated were not put right.

So the false prophet cries, "Let's all be pals together, and forget our little differences!" The true prophet warns that deep beneath the apparent harmony are moral choices still unmade, balancing truths still unstated, and the health of society requires them to be brought to light and squarely faced. Those who take this road will undoubtedly be scorned as dismal Jeremiahs. But it is worth remembering that Jeremiah proved to be right and those who did not listen to him perished.

4. *False prophets speak a simple word of Promise or Judgment: true prophets speak a paradoxical word of Promise and Judgment.*

When the Hebrew prophets tried to puzzle out what God was saying to their nation, they discovered a strange thing about his mode of address. He spoke always a word of promise which offered fulfillment and a satisfying destiny, but if the people seized the promise and forgot the terms on which it was offered, that same word was transformed by their disobedience into judgment. Yet even when the faithless nation was carried off captive and suffered a terrible fate at the hands of strangers, the prophets at least never made the mistake of thinking that God's word of judgment had canceled out his original promise, or else his ultimate purposes could not be achieved. And so on the far side of tragedy, whilst they still lay deep in judgment, the Jews heard a new promise, "Babylon is fallen!"

So the truly prophetic word has moral depth. It is never flippant or casually simple because it is addressed to man, who oscillates between extremes of pride and humility, misery and grandeur. And this word speaks of promise *and* judgment, because man needs both to be jolted into a sense of dignity when he is groveling in the dust and knocked off his perch when he gets cocky and forgets he is human.

False prophets, whose interpretation of life is always neat and tidy, will not wrestle with the ambiguities of this paradoxical word, and so they abolish its depth, tear apart the two halves, and become soothsayers of either unmitigated doom or unalloyed bliss. They speak a simple word of promise that fills men with unwarranted optimism or a simple word of judgment which drives them into irredeemable despair.

49

For instance, successive presidents of the United States have proved falsely prophetic about Vietnam and ignored the darker dimensions of the war. They have spoken a word of promise without judgment—confident predictions that victory would be won this year, next year, the year after; exclamations of satisfaction that communism was being contained in Asia and that soon the boys would be able to come home. And so unwonted optimism lured the United States deeper and deeper into the morass until they were entangled almost beyond extrication. Had promise been balanced by judgment, the nation might have been prepared for the moral harrowing it was to undergo, and due warning that such an engagement must bleed not only its manpower but its very soul could have blown sanity and political realism through the corridors of power.

Or consider the opposite case. The "Keep Britain White" agitators are false prophets because they are offering a word of judgment without promise. They are chilling the nation's blood with their prognostications about the horrid consequences of continued Commonwealth immigration and blinding themselves to the possibility of the enrichment of a tired, gray national life by the injection of some of the color and culture of other races.

Jesus must be our model here. All his breathtaking promises embodied judgment because each one concluded with an unspoken *"but if not"*! And yet his harshest judgments offered men promise for they were aimed at bringing them to the point of a contrition which destroyed their pride without extinguishing their hope. That is the essence of true prophecy—a word of judgment which leads men to repentance and yet embodies promise, the assurance that forgiveness is possible.

5. *False prophets are content to speak: true prophets also act.*
Action is always superior to speech in the Gospels, which

is why the Word became flesh and not newsprint. Jesus did not harangue men on the dignity of labor: he worked at a carpenter's bench. He didn't talk much about immortality: he raised the dead. He didn't give a course of lectures on the value of human personality: he made friends with publicans and sinners. He didn't write a thesis on the primacy of the spiritual over the material: he walked on water. He didn't construct theologies of heaven and hell: he put a glass of water at the focal point. He didn't tell them: he showed them.

The world is surfeited with words, and false prophets are producing more than their share. But we fight them on their own ground and merely add to the din when we match them speech for speech and argument for argument. The words of the false prophet can only be confounded by the actions of the true prophet. Much of the wrangling about race relations in Britain, for example, is so much wasted time. If every time false prophets made speeches warning of the dangers of close contact between the races, true prophets went out and made friends with another colored family, the perfect answer to a false case would have been made.

Maybe the world is saying to the church: Don't tell us, show us! Thomas is the patron saint of our age; until men can touch the marks of suffering, they will not believe, and knowing the extent to which false messiahs bawling their wares and nostrums have turned the earth into another Tower of Babel, who is to blame them?

To show them rather than tell them requires a transformation of the prophetic personality. The old prophet was a talented individualist: the new prophet is a community of people in which hope has been made visible—a community whose spirit is so open, accepting, and forgiving that none with eyes to see can doubt that at least a bit of the bad old world has been changed into God's new creation.

So in each of these ways, every one of God's people is a prophet—or he's a dead loss!

CHAPTER 5

Before Winter

"Do your best to come quickly. Come before winter."
II Timothy 4:21.

Anyone who has lived in the tropics knows that there is a quickening of the pace of life, a growing sense of urgency just before the rains set in. People say, "We must get this, that, or the other thing done before the rains!" because they know that once those torrential storms sweep down, communication is difficult, roads and bridges are swept away, valleys and plains are flooded, and life generally gets bogged down in mud until the rains stop.

There is a little phrase in Paul's second letter to Timothy which breathes this same sense of urgency. Paul is in a Roman jail, a dying man. He is a man with only three close friends—the unseen Master whom he served, his physician, Luke, and Timothy, a young Hebrew-Greek half-caste whom he has left in charge of the church at Ephesus. So he writes to Timothy asking him to come to Rome, and to bring with him his books and his old travel-stained robe. To this summons, he adds a postscript, "Do your best to come quickly. Come before winter!"

Why before winter? Presumably because once winter set in, the Mediterranean became unnavigable; those bitter gales would cut Paul and Timothy off from each other until the spring, and Paul has a feeling in his bones that he will not be around when the sea routes open up again.

Before winter or never. There are some things in this life which will never get done if they are not done before winter. The return of spring will garland the graves of opportunities ungrasped and hopes that can never be realized. There are certain doors now open that winter will slam shut. There are certain voices to which we can now respond which winter may silence forever. For instance:

The Voice of the Other

If Timothy had dallied, he would have arrived in Rome when the winter was over to find his friend silent in the ground. Some of the saddest words ever penned were inscribed by Thomas Carlyle over his wife's grave at the Old Kirk, Haddington: "Oh, that I had you with me yet for five minutes by my side that I might tell you all." But whatever Thomas Carlyle had left unsaid, his wife was never to hear. The winter had intervened.

It is this realization that winter *must* come that injects urgency into all our human relationships. Jesus warned his disciples, "The poor you always have with you, but I shall not be with you always"—so, if there's something you want to ask, ask it now; if there's something you don't understand, now's the time to get to the bottom of it; if you have any request to make, make it now! Before winter.

How often do we exclaim, "What! Old Jack gone? I saw him only last week in town!" Possibly there was something we had to say to Old Jack; a breach to be healed; words of apology or encouragement to be spoken; maybe we just wanted to shake his hand. But the onset of winter has mocked our good intentions. The ultimate frustration in this life is to struggle to put into words something that must be said in order that we may have peace of mind, and then when we get round to it, find that the Other is forever beyond the range of our voice.

When the Other calls out, answer now, not tomorrow or next week or on your birthday. Now. Before winter.

The Voice of Social Conscience

One of the most depressing lessons to be derived from the study of history is the realization that men just do not learn from their past mistakes. Our town and village war memorials with their twin lists of dead remind us that not one but two generations were wiped off the earth by a repetition of the same terrifying combination of bumbling incompetence, greed, and thirst for revenge. The Americans are now hopelessly bogged down in an enervating war in Vietnam because they did not learn the lesson of the French debacle there in 1954. The Russians march back into Prague in 1968 to repeat the rape of Czechoslovakia which sparked off the Cold War in 1948.

International and social tensions unresolved, wounds unhealed, problems unsolved—multiply by a kind of geometric progression so that an issue hardens into a situation, a new development becomes a fact of life. Yet there is a tide in the affairs of men, a moment which can be seized before nations slide into disaster. Rhodesia is possibly the best example in our time. There was a point when Britain still had the initiative, when firm action and resolution might well have prevented Rhodesia's unilateral declaration of independence. But she havered and winter overtook her, and now it is too late; she is impotent to heal a running sore likely to afflict southern Africa for generations.

Consider an illustration from Britain's domestic life—the challenge of the colored immigrants amongst us. They are not, as is often claimed, an intractable problem; they are an enriching presence. There is still time to respond, not negatively with immigration quotas and restrictive legislation, but positively by molding our social structures to take account of them, by educating our children to be color-blind, by establishing relationships with them that can withstand the inevitable tensions of the color-encounter. Still time, but not much, to respond to the voice of social conscience. But ignore them and hope they will go away, and our children's children will find themselves like our American cousins struggling to clean up the accumulated mess of generations.

Across the full spectrum of social and political issues there are areas where we still have the initiative; where we are one jump ahead of events. But if we don't act before winter, things will harden and solidify, attitudes will become rigid, and we shall fall victim to our own indolence. Twice in the Garden of Gethsemane Jesus tried to wake his disciples. The third time, he said, "Sleep on!" Sleep on—an irretrievable opportunity had been lost to be present at the decisive crisis of history. How often in our time has God been forced to tell us, "Sleep on!" Winter has come and we were not prepared.

The Voice of a Second Chance

The human personality undergoes strange fluxes. Sometimes we are sensitive, malleable, teachable; at other times we are hard, resistant, deaf to the voice of reason. There are crisis points in our lives just as there is a critical temperature in the molding of metal when it is neither too hard nor too fluid to be shaped at will. But let the temperature drop or rise by a few degrees and nothing can be done with it; the whole process is abortive.

God gives every man a second chance to redeem himself, to make a fresh start, to halt a disastrous drift, but the timing of that critical point is his secret. At some time in our journey through life our path takes us past that pool where, on unpredictable occasions, an angel troubles the waters. Step in then and we can be healed, but wait until the ripples subside and it is too late.

We talk as though it were easy to sin and hard to be good. To some extent that is our melancholy experience. Yet there is always one final defense to be surmounted before we can throw off all restraints—it may take the form of an image to be erased from our memories or a voice to be drowned; that voice of a second chance which urges us that it is still not too late; we can scramble back before the trickle of stones becomes an avalanche. You see this most clearly in all forms of addiction. There is a moment when some inner voice seems to say, "This is your hour! Conquer this thing now and you will be its master forever. Delay, and you are lost!"

None of us is entirely without self-insight. All but the most insensitive know when we are approaching some point of no return. But because we are not always malleable, open-eyed, awake, it is dangerous to leave matters so that we face an ultimate crisis when we are at our most stubborn and unteachable. If a fresh start is indicated *and we know it*— now is the time. Before winter.

The Voice of God

Though I have explored the political and social dimensions of the Christian faith as much as most ministers, I have never lost my sense of the centrality of Christian conversion. The church which does not preach it has no gospel and the church which does not reap the harvest of it is blindly disobedient.

Yet it seems to me that this experience is more complex, and indeed mysterious, than some mass evangelists would have us believe. It is not to be had on demand like a pack of cigarettes from a vending machine nor is it cosy, easy, or slick. The motivating factor is the grace of God, which must always be humanly unpredictable. It cannot be demanded, commanded, or deserved. There are times when God speaks and times when he is silent, which is why the New Testament says that vigilance is the essential precondition of faith. "No man," warned Jesus, "knows the hour," so those who would be saved are commanded to live always in the *now* of expectation so that when the Bridegroom comes, they are not caught napping.

Nor is it only the individual Christian who must sometimes

endure the dark night of the soul when the heavens seem closed up and life drags on without zest or flavor. The church, too, has its wilderness experiences where it treks through the desert without the encouragement of unearthly visions or heavenly voices: just sun, sand, and distance. Much of our pessimism about the prospects for the Christian faith and even our radical doubts about God's existence are products of these arid stretches of life. And to stay awake in the absence of landmarks calls for a quality of dogged persistence which is the fruit of a hard disciplining of the will. This is the contemporary experience of the church, and it is hardly surprising that casualties are falling by the way in growing numbers.

But the church's survival as a miracle of hope against experience has been made possible by those in its ranks who were still alert when the totally unexpected occurred—springs of water in the desert, shafts of light in the dark—and those who *saw*, the visionaries of the faith, have nerved the rest to stagger on.

There is nothing very *cosy* about that account of Christian experience, but I believe it to be realistic and to embody a warning that we had better seize the opportunity of getting into training before winter, or if winter is already upon us, to take advantage of its unseasonably bright days.

Every Christian lives at the focal point of two pressures. One is the urgency of God's purposes. Martin Luther put it well when he wrote, "The Word of God is as a shower of rain that never returns where once it has been. The Greeks had it, but it passed over. The Romans and the Jews had it, but it passed over. Seize it whoever can. You must not think you have it for ever!" It is a jolt to our complacency as a church in those times when we reflect smugly that God cannot do without us to remember that Jesus said God could turn stones into sons of Abraham. If we fail to do the job he has laid upon us, then he will find some other instrument of his will, and we

57

shall be left high and dry like the rusting equipment of some long-abandoned experiment.

The other pressure upon us is created by the uncertainty of human life. David said to Jonathan, "There is but one step between me and death." There is only one step between any of us and death. An old rabbi was asked by his disciples when a man ought to make his peace with God. He reflected for a moment, then replied, "A man ought to make his peace with God one minute before he dies." "But, Master," they protested, "we haven't the foggiest idea when we shall die!" "Exactly," said the Rabbi. "So do it now!"

Do it now. Before winter.

CHAPTER 6

The Realm of a Deathless Yes

"Jesus . . . was not Yes and No; but in him it is always Yes. For all the promises of God find their Yes in him."
II Corinthians 1:19, 20.

The politicians' stock stands pretty low with ordinary people at the present moment. A long time ago Shakespeare called them "glass-eyed." "Get thee glass eyes: and like a scurvy politician, seem to see things thou dost not!" So there's nothing particularly novel in the popular accusation that politicians are purveyors of false promises and prone to speak with forked tongues. We sneer, "Ask them *any* question and you'll get the same reply—Yes *and* No, with reservations on both sides!" But it is just possible that those politicians who are men of integrity have learned through hard experience that there are few important questions which can be answered with an unequivocal yes or no. Truth may lie more in the vaguer areas of Yes-But, or No-And-Yet.

Paul seems to show sympathy with this dilemma of the politicians when he claims that life is a blend of Yes and No. We probably would not express it so profoundly, but this insight sheds light upon our experience.

THE REALM OF YES AND NO

All natural life stands upon this law of Yes and No. Not Yes alone or No alone. But Yes and No held together in tension. Whatever can be truly said about the world of men is never simple; it is a counterpoint of denials and affirmations. Over the labyrinth of life-directions, which we have the freedom to explore, there hang no constant green or constant red lights, but lights which flash green one moment and red the next.

Take *human relationships*. They stand under this law. All human encounters are of the stop-go variety. A Yes is sounded over our desire to get to know someone better, but at a certain point this Yes will almost certainly shade into No—a shutter comes down to keep us out of some inner sanctum of privacy. Indeed, the depth of a relationship can be measured by the distance one can travel "into" another person before the Yes becomes muffled and finally clarifies in No. Most dilemmas of relationship arise from this blurred area where Yes appears about to change to No. We say, "We don't know where we are with X!" And we are afraid to move forward for fear of presumption lest we betray a trust.

The classical Yes in everyday life is the one said by a girl to the man who proposes to her. Unless she is remarkably single-minded or suffering from overactive glands and an underactive brain, her Yes has embodied and finally overcome a whole range of No's—hesitations, doubts, uncertainties. And if her judgment proves unsound, one or more of those No's may eventually rise up and choke out the original Yes so that the relationship dies.

Take *the search for truth*. This stands under the law of Yes and No. If a pilot, wanting to fly from A to B, measures his course with strict accuracy on a good map with a reliable computer and then flies it with great care, he will end up miles away from his desired destination. A whole series of factors such as wind drift and magnetic variation will turn his theoretical truth into actual error. Talking about political truth, Reinhold Niebuhr has said, "There is an element of truth in some positions which becomes falsehood precisely when it is carried through too consistently." Fascism is a good example of what happens when men get hold of a truth about the state and follow it through so rigorously that it turns into monstrous error—Yes becoming No.

Or consider a foolish theologian who decides to give a lecture about God which is strictly theoretical in the sense that he will not take into account his own or the church's experience of God. It is to be a symphony of pure logic. But because God is the object of faith, nothing we can say about him has the character of scientific certainty. So the theologian begins by making a statement about God which has, let's say for argument's sake, a 90 percent chance of being true. From this statement he derives a whole series of other statements about God, each one of which depends for its truth on the one that preceded it. His final statement will not have a probability of 90 percent, as his first had. Mathematically, the probability that his final statement is true may be as low as 25 percent. Thus, without any intentional human error, the predominantly Yes has been transformed into the predominantly No.

Take *the search for God*. This stands under the law of Yes and No. From the beginning of time, men have tried to fight their way toward heaven. All kinds of promising paths have opened up—a Yes has sounded over the rites of sacrifice, the observances of religious ceremonial, or the way of personal renunciation. And so these spiritual explorers have founded their religions, led new movements, or publicized their teachings, the way to God at long last revealed! But the devotees who have stuck closest to the rules and gone farthest along the road charted by their *gurus* have made the disconcerting discovery that the goal recedes all the while they try to reach it. Yes has given way to a No which effectively bars the way to God; a No which preserves God's infinite distance from man.

That experience of spiritual aridity called by the saints the dark night of the soul has been known to take hold of the religiously self-righteous and sound a blank No that damns the cocky Yes of their previous superficial spiritual exuberance. It is a jarring jolt to those cheerful chappies of any faith

61

who claim to have a matey, back-slapping approach to God and who speak with arrogant certitude about him on the basis of some private intelligence he has whispered in their ear. It took Martin Luther a long time to realize that the Yes which sent him to join the Augustinian Hermits at Erfurt had changed into a No that not all the flagellation and self-denial could cancel out. The way to God was barred.

Man's age-old search for God stands under this law of Yes and No.

Take *the certainty of earthly mortality*. Here the law of Yes and No is most poignantly demonstrated. Life sounds a resounding Yes to a man—his gifts and potentialities and powers—then just as the world is poised to reap the harvest of achievement, a sudden shocking No drowns out the Yes, and he is taken from us. So we lose a William Temple, a John F. Kennedy, a Martin Luther King; so we lose any man or woman who enriches the world, however slightly. The Yes which we interpret according to our personal philosophy as the smile of fortune, the promptings of destiny, or divinely ordained vocation expires with a sigh leaving a silence pregnant with an ultimate No.

Death's No puts terminus to life's bravest Yes.

There are those who cannot bear the burden of this law of Yes and No. They hate ambiguity and want life to give them a straight answer—Yes or No. So they tear into two pieces that banner flying over life upon which is emblazoned this strange law and nail to their mast whichever half suits them best. Some with brave optimism look for a way of life which seems to offer a Yes without any balancing No. Religiously, they are to be counted amongst those who, in Richard Niebuhr's epigram, want to believe in a Christ without a cross, who brings men without sin into a kingdom without judgment. Politically, they end up making a god of the state as the fascist does, or of an ideology as the communist does, or of simple goodwill as the humanitarian does. With a limitless capacity for self-delusion, they try to deal with life's darker realities the way the Christian Scientist deals with disease—by steadfastly refusing to acknowledge its existence. But sooner or later, their naïveté or arrogance brings them crashing. The No they have struggled to suppress rises to choke the life out of their pathetic Yes.

Others resolve to become life-deniers. Tired of being tantalized by the interplay of Yes and No, they accept the worst and turn it into a philosophy. They abandon all hope and human expectations. For them, the Buddhist *stupa*—the bubble—is the appropriate symbol for a life that is ephemeral and futile. There are Christians with a streak of perverted puritanism in them who say No to life and hope to preserve their virtue in the same way a swimmer tries to keep his clothes dry, by avoiding plunging into the water. And there are thousands of ordinary folk who have been hurt by someone, and having decided that every new affection brings a new affliction, they live behind closed doors, psychological or actual, to avoid human encounter. The result is cynicism, despair, and deadness. You can pretend that there is no Yes at life's heart just as you can pretend that there is no sun at the center of the solar system, but the result is likely to be the same in both cases—the determined flight from reality that leads to the madhouse.

THE REALM OF A DEATHLESS YES

No clearer possible Yes could have been sounded than over Jesus of Nazareth. His life was one of boundless horizons in healing, teaching, and service. Yet even this sublime Yes was drowned by the ultimate No of Calvary. And all man's hopes of breaking out of this vicious circle were buried with him in a tomb.

Then on the third day, he rose from the dead. Another Yes had been sounded beyond the Yes and No of natural life. God said Yes to his obedience, Yes to his goodness,

Yes to his sense of oneness with the source of all being. And God's Yes is not balanced by any No. It is a final Yes which, coming from *beyond* history, but sounding *within* history, cannot be vitiated or modified. So as Paul puts it—in Jesus it is always Yes, every contingent No has been canceled out. And those who are alive with his life are also drawn into this realm of a deathless Yes.

1. In Jesus, Yes has sounded to a knowledge of God not barred by any No.

The present theological ferment of our time is only possible because this Yes has sounded. Words like heresy and ortho-doxy now have a quaintly old-fashioned ring in many areas of the church. Theology has ceased to be the exclusive purview of the professional expert—Latin theses have given way to paperbacks. The solicitous concern of the clergy to avoid exposing the laity to so-called difficult theological ques-tions is now seen for what it is, a relic of medieval priestly freemasonry, where the justification for the parson's existence at all was the possession of a body of arcane knowledge de-nied to the ordinary man. This "not in front of the chil-dren!" attitude of some clergy is being swept aside in scorn partly because many lay folk are now better educated than their parson, and also because the advent of the mass media has rendered suspect all ideas which are meant for general consumption but which cannot be communicated directly to the public in an idiom they can understand. And there is a growing feeling in the church that *any* truths about God which are too difficult for the man in the pew to grasp have no value anyway except in those closed circles where professors chase the tails of their academic gowns.

Now because something is happening on such a wide scale, this does not mean that it is necessarily good; but this new freedom to explore God is so consonant with the spirit of Jesus that it must be right. God's Yes to our search for him means that we can start from any point and take any route that is congenial to us. The resurgence of Eastern cults, the growing strength of mystical movements, the ethical involvement in great issues of the day by humanists who choose to make man their road to God—all these and many more explorations into divinity have been made possible by the explosion into life of the resurrection power of Jesus, even though his name is never invoked. Let popes hurl their anathemas and fundamentalists scream damnation, God's endorsement of Jesus as the best human model of the inner connection between truth, love, and joy has opened doors that the combined weights of all the inquisitions and ecclesiastical vested interests can never again force closed.

The illustration may be an infantile one, but God's Yes to Jesus has transformed man's situation from that of the chastened boy standing on the far side of his headmaster's desk to that of a child climbing all over his father. "Go ahead!" says God, "I'm not afraid of the truth. Why should you be?"

Supremely, of course, this knowledge of himself to which God says Yes is summarized in Jesus. We cannot know what God is like, but we do know what a God-filled man is like. The New Testament writers, with the two exceptions in Romans 9:5 and Hebrews 1:8, never claimed that Jesus *was* God, but that God was uniquely at work in him to such a degree that when men rejected him, they rejected God. The vast volumes of historical theology with their thousands of pages of discussion of the so-called heresies about the person and work of Jesus show that the study of Jesus is inexhaustible. About this Galilean peasant more books have been written and more words spoken than about anyone else in the history of the world. They are but a fraction of the total response to that Yes God sounded in Jesus. And the exploration will go on until the end of time. No one, no group or school or faculty or church, will ever get to the bottom of Jesus. God would not endorse one whose significance could be exhausted so easily that men were left at a loose end, looking around for other messiahs. This Yes beyond history must encompass the whole of history or it would be subject to the law of Yes and No under which all natural life stands.

2. *In Jesus, Yes has sounded to relationships which are not restricted by any No.*

That statement could be taken as an endorsement of the permissive society, the new morality, that spirit of our time which the orthodox parody as "to blazes with the Ten Commandments! Let everyone do what the hell he likes!" But we must risk the wrath of the Pharisees amongst us to stand for a new openness to the demands upon us of our fellow human beings which are governed not by any law or code of ethics, but solely in terms of what love demands. Such an approach to human relationships, far from encouraging self-indulgence and expressing self-will as the legalists claim, demands much greater self-discipline. We cannot hide behind the rules, warping our personalities in fancied obedience to some higher law or doing the right thing with a bad grace because we "ought to." God's Yes in Jesus to open human encounter puts the ball squarely in our court and lays upon us the ultimate responsibility for the other's welfare. Hardly a "Cassanova's Charter," to use in a different context Baroness Summerskill's description of the new divorce bill in Britain!

John Robinson put it well in *Honest to God:* "Love alone, because, as it were, it has a built-in moral compass enabling it to 'home' intuitively upon the deepest need of the other, can allow itself to be directed completely by the situation. It alone can afford to be utterly open to the situation, or rather the person in the situation, uniquely and for his own sake, without losing its direction and conditionality." Isn't this precisely how Jesus behaved in his determination that compassion for persons must override all laws? So he commended David for eating the sacred bread of the temple;

so he broke the sabbath in order to heal. Human hunger and human suffering created their own ethic beyond the stated rules.

Jesus has made possible a quality of relationship in which we may say Yes to the other, unconditionally, guided only by what love requires. And over such relationships No does not sound, for when we must restrain ourselves, we do so not because we have heard the No of the law's prohibition but the Yes of love's requirements.

3. *In Jesus, Yes has sounded to a kind of truth which is not neutralized by error.*

This truth is not speculation or earthly wisdom. It is not even that healthy contention described by Betrand Russell: "In matter of opinion it is a good thing if there is a vigorous discussion between different schools of thought. In the mental world there is everything to be said in favor of a struggle for existence, leading with luck to a survival of the fittest." This truth which is not balanced by error is the saving truth of the gospel. It is Yes without No because it can be trusted; one may bank one's life upon it. It is free from illusions and distortions.

There is no "on balance" or "taking this into account or that" about it. It is truth which is meant to be done. There is that daring verb in John 3:21," He who *does* the truth comes to the light." This obviously means more than doing what seems to be the right thing; that is a course of action. This verse is talking about a way of life—sharing the life of the one over whom God's Yes of truth has sounded. This is truth which is intended to make us free—delivered from every bondage, either to law which may be a pale reflection of the truth or to doctrines which can only point to the truth.

It is truth which short-circuits all the endless checks and balances and qualifications that lie along the road to its discovery. The opposite of this saving truth of the gospel is not the *opinion* of a Greek thought nor the *lie* of moralism but *nothingness*, chaos, a thing of dust and ashes. For the gospel is not a series of propositions or a body of teaching but a cold statement of how all the laws of God find their fulfillment in Jesus; how God has delivered the keys of the kingdom to him and how God has chosen that we be saved or judged by this man. God alone knows why he should do things this way, and he isn't telling. But there is no error in the gospel for the same reason there is no error in a man's red hair or a shower of rain or the wetness of water. It is the way things *are*. And to deny the way things are is not to perpetuate an error but to embrace insanity.

4. *In Jesus, God says Yes to a life beyond death.*

This ultimate No of mortality cannot be sounded over Jesus because he already has his death behind him. Resurrection life is the realm of a deathless Yes. For those who share in the power of Jesus' resurrection, their deaths too, in all but the biological sense, are behind them. For them, death *is* a biological crisis, but it is not a spiritual one. Between a man's baptism or his conversion and the summation of all things, the judgment, if you like—provided you do not garnish that truth with crude and misleading imagery—there is no interruption of the development and pace of life either at the point of physical dissolution or at any other time.

It is understandable that men should fear death. Would we not equally have been terrified of birth if some obstetrician could have communicated with us in the womb and given us a clinical description of what was about to happen to us, hour by hour? But we must not judge the significance of any occurrence by the extent of our fear of it. The simple affirmation, "God is love," involves in its endless facets one that gives the lie to the cruciality of death as an ultimate crisis. Love is the drive to unite all that is separated, in time, in place, in condition. It is the lynch-pin of the unity of all creation and, therefore, cannot be fulfilled within the tiny span of existence between a man's birth and death. There are many forms of separation which cannot be overcome in that space of time—so man meets his death, an unfinished creature. But he has been given the gift of love, and that cannot be taken from him. The infinite has been joined to the finite; the work of uniting us to the source of all being has begun, and we know it has begun not because we see heavenly visions or hear heavenly voices but because in practical, down-to-earth situations we can give and receive love. Why else did John write, "We know we have passed from death to life because we love the brethren"? Paul's statement that *nothing* can separate us from the love of God—"neither life nor death nor things present nor things to come"—is not so much an assurance of some kind of mystical union with God as a simple declaration that we last as long as love lasts, and love lasts as long as God's love lasts—which is presumably a very long time!

Although the New Testament is explicit about the reality of eternal life, it is agnostic about the mechanics of it, so it would not be a good idea to labor this point. It is enough to claim that those who share the resurrection life of Jesus pass into the realm of a deathless Yes which cannot be canceled out by any No.

GOD'S YES AND MAN'S YES

Paul goes on to affirm that all the promises of God find their Yes in Jesus. This means two things, I think. The first is that the totality of what God has to say to man has been summed up in Jesus. All the long record of his dealings with men through countless centuries, all the body of teaching and law passed on to, or discovered by, seers and prophets and visionaries of many lands and ages, have been reduced to manageable proportions in Jesus—in just the same way that a mountain of documents and miles of statistics can be compressed into the size of a computer card. If you are not the scholarly, reflective sort of person, you may with a clear conscience walk past all the libraries of religion and spiritual learning and settle for the truth incarnate in the personality of Jesus.

Secondly, if all the promises of God find their Yes in Jesus, this must mean that God undertakes to honor every promise Jesus gave to men.

"I have told them," says Jesus, "that if they have the faith of a grain of mustard seed they can move mountains!" "Yes," says God . . .

"I have told them," says Jesus, "that I will be with them to the end of time!" "Yes," says God . . .

"I have told them that those who live in me will never die!" "Yes," says God.

All the promises of God finding their Yes in Jesus means that his breathtaking claims were not the ravings of a madman nor the stabs in the dark of a pious fool. He had authority to offer those promises, and in the experience of Paul and the early church, God had honored every one of them.

It is, I suppose, the greatest proof of man's dignity and freedom that all the light and power of this realm of the deathless Yes can only be unlocked if he is willing to respond to God's great Yes with his own simple Yes. Then that law of Yes and No under which we all stand in history is not abolished but transcended. But the Yes beyond Yes and No cannot be sounded without our permission. It is the tremendous echo throughout the universe of our own hesitant affirmation.

It is quite a thought; just how much hangs upon that tiny word—Yes—both in this life and beyond.

CHAPTER 7

Mankind My Church

"Consider what is the breadth and length and depth of the love
of God."   Ephesians 3:18.

One of the hopeful features of our time is the growing
amount of shared concern amongst people of many faiths
and ideologies about the great scourges of mankind—hunger,
discrimination, injustice, and war. Sit in a meeting to discuss
overseas aid and you will probably find a Young Liberal on
one side of you and a Marxist on the other. Join a protest
march and it may well be a humanist or Maoist who helps
you to carry the banner. Chain yourself to the railings outside 10 Downing Street and you are quite likely to pass the
time of day with a little old lady from Surbiton on the end
of the next chain who is protesting against the ill-treatment
of circus animals. And God knows who will be occupying
the next cell if they haul you off to the police station!

Now because the concerns of so many people of goodwill
coincide with our own, we must not make the error of claiming
that they are all Christians but don't know it. Imagine the explosion if the *Morning Star* announced that some Conservative alderman in Cheam was a Communist but didn't know it!
When a man has fought his way through to the humanist
position, rejecting the claims of Christianity on the way, it is
an insult to his integrity to suggest that he really is a Christian
but hasn't got round to finding it out yet. We may think we
are paying him a compliment: he will probably take it as
evidence of our arrogance or sloppy-mindedness.

Short of baptizing all our allies into the faith, is it possible
to go further than joint action on specific issues? Since we

already have a common conscience, is it possible to reach a common mind—affirmations we can make together without betraying the integrity of whatever faith we separately hold? Let me propose three such affirmations which are at least a program for debate. I have put them within the framework of Paul's statement about the extent of God's love not because I think any of them is *identical* with the particular dimension to which I relate it, but because, from the Christian angle, it is the majestic proportions of God's love which offer me the freedom to thrust out and meet other men's minds.

Firstly, as to the breadth of the love of God:
I believe in one church, and that church is mankind.

A friend of mine is fond of saying when he is exasperated, "I *like* the human race. All my family belong to it and some of my wife's family as well!" Fair enough as an affectionate gibe at one's mother-in-law, but in a more serious idiom, it expresses an attitude which is at the root of many of our political and religious problems. All my fellow whites belong to the chosen people, and some blacks as well! All Methodists are part of a true church, and a few Catholics as well!

I've been doing some homework on this word *church*. The English word is derived from a Greek one which means "house of the Lord"—a good, safe, religious concept. But according to Paul Minear, over eighty different words for *church* are to be found in the Bible, and *that* is not one of them. I like *ecclesia* best. It was pinched from the politicians and means simply "an assembly of the people"—all of them, the good, bad, and indifferent—for law-giving, for war and play and talk. The word's meaning has changed a lot in its transmission through time, of course, but originally it must have been inclusive, open, and accepting in spirit.

What have we done to this vision of all-embracing community that our *ecclesia* should have become badges of our

72

exclusiveness? I am a Methodist and, therefore, not an Anglican; a Protestant and, therefore, not a Catholic; a Christian and, therefore, not a Jew. For all the gusto with which I bellow forth my positive beliefs, it is the things that mark me off from others that are, in the eyes of the world, the easiest way of identifying me.

But it won't do. I am more than a Methodist, more than a Protestant; yes, more even than a Christian. I am first and foremost a member of the human race, and to that must be my primary allegiance. So I have only one *ecclesia*—mankind. There is only one true baptism, which is birth, and only one true sacramental table—at which every member of the human race will some day sit by right *and be fed!* Every other so-called sacrament is a parody of these true sacraments, just as our institutional churches are a parody of the true *ecclesia*.

Is this conviction of mine thinly veiled humanism? I think not, because I take with the utmost seriousness two theological realities which the true humanist would deny. I have talked about them elsewhere[1]—they are the radical nature of sin and the operation in human life of the grace of God as a creative factor which does not emerge naturally from man's own makeup or social arrangements. Only an analysis and a program which take account of both these factors has any hope of being able to match up to the size of the problems which face mankind.

Am I then preaching some kind of universalism—the belief that all men in the end must be saved? It doesn't seem to me that it is any of my business to make judgments of that magnitude. There are those who, wrapping the vestments of their ecclesiastical or biblical authority around them, feel qualified to pronounce on such matters. I wish them well. I would as soon play with forked lightning as try to lay down the law about the eternal destiny of any man. If there is a boundary between faith and unfaith running somewhere

[1] See above, pp. 34-35.

through the community of men, only God knows where it is. No mortal man has the right to draw such a line and so set himself up as a judge over his fellowmen. How the "saved" are divided from the "damned" is God's business; but I have a feeling in my bones that it will not be according to our elaborate schemes of salvation. It is because our existing *ecclesia* are such monuments to our egotism and censoriousness that we imagine God is bound by our prejudices—saving those we invite to join us and damning those we cast out.

One thing I am sure about. Jesus is a member of this *ecclesia* which embraces all mankind; no other *ecclesia* is big enough to hold him. He is the one who by definition puts himself on the other side of any barrier, fence, or frontier we erect to safeguard what is our own or even what we think is his. Because he is the great outsider, that invisible line round the church we would claim marks Christians off from non-Christians effectively keeps him out also. For Jesus was not a Christian: he was a man. And if the gospel makes any sense at all, it is with man he will take his stand, any man, who is excluded from the feast of life.

Nor do I think that my conviction about the nature of the true *ecclesia* can be dismissed as hopeless idealism. It is not a dream but a crusade. It is a steadfast refusal to give ultimate value to anything, however worthy it may be in itself, that cuts me off from my fellowmen. And it is a determination to strengthen whatever ties bind me to all the rest of humanity. The world which so often in our day seems to be preaching the gospel to the church is, I am sure, feeling after this sense of wholeness. You see it in the minor commerce of living— take a recent report which announced that there are over 70,000 registered charities in Britain alone. I do not think this is just evidence of vapid humanitarianism or maudlin sentimentality. I think that ordinary people, frustrated by their inability to get any closer to the victims of life the whole world over, are demonstrating their solidarity the only way they know—by popping sixpences in a box to forge a link with a starving Nigerian or a Vietnamese refugee or a nameless political prisoner in eastern Europe. Certainly it is not enough. We do not discharge our responsibility to the less fortunate by a charitable hand-out. But it is a beginning. The shadowy dimensions of God's *ecclesia* are graven across the sky in a thousand isolated signs.

The two great enemies of God's *ecclesia* are blind patriotism and religious exclusiveness. Certainly I can know God within the confines of my own communion—but only a bit of him. Certainly I can love my neighbor in my own land—but only a few of them. Is it not significant that in that vision of the New Jerusalem described in Revelation, it is specifically stated that there is to be found there "neither Temples nor Sword"? No church. No state.

Theologians warn us against the danger of identifying the church with the kingdom of God. The church, says one, is only the scaffolding of the kingdom. So be it. Then might it not be wise to think in terms of a scaffolding, an *ecclesia*, which makes some pretension to being big enough to contain the final structure? What would we say of an engineer who started out to build a skyscraper using the rudimentary scaffolding suited to supporting the corner teashop? We must be careful not to be misled by metaphor. The concept of "bigness" is irrelevant in that image of the kingdom as a grain of mustard seed growing secretly. It is quality, not quantity; a vitamin and not roughage. But within history at least, men must live within structures of some kind, and if a new heaven and a new earth is on the cards at all, do you see the Methodist Church or even all the churches added together providing an adequate scaffolding for such a tremendous conception? Nothing of man's devising *could*, but we ought to be working and planning and praying within the context of an *ecclesia* which is some match for the grandeur of the vision.

75

The truth is that we need the wealth and gifts of all mankind to be brought to bear upon the problems which preoccupy any part of it. Even the recovery of theological power within the church depends upon our willingness to draw upon sources much wider than the Christian tradition. Missionaries who go out, on fire to convert the heathen, are returning home in growing numbers with their faith strengthened and clarified by the impact upon them of other great religions. Have we not got a fresh view of Jesus by the abandonment of the old harsh proselytizing of the Jews in favor of the recognition that Christianity and Judaism are two faiths with a common center; that every Christian is, in a manner of speaking, an honorary Jew?

My own experience supports this conviction. It has taken a cross-section of humanity to demonstrate the riches of Christ. An African nationalist movement showed me what the fellowship of the Holy Spirit might mean; a Buddhist monk in Saigon taught me what the burning charity of Christ looks like in action; an American atheist always comes to mind when I think of that quality of integrity on fire Jesus called "doing the truth."

The breadth of God's love encourages us to explore what it means to be part of God's great *ecclesia*—not the one stamped on our membership cards but that graven on our souls. And if you say, as you may well, that talk about one's *ecclesia* being mankind is much too vague, I can only retort that there is more truth in a reality that defies definition than in a definition devoid of reality—and our institutional churches seem to have got perilously close to that point.

Secondly, as to the length of the love of God:
It is necessary to stand for things that will not come to pass until long after we are gone.

One of my treasured possessions is a faded newspaper clipping on which is a photograph of Betrand Russell at a very advanced age being marched off to jail for his part in a demonstration against nuclear weapons. Now whether he was right or wrong on the specific policy issue is beside the point; the intriguing question is: Why did he bother? Why was he getting steamed up about something which couldn't possibly affect him personally? He must have known that he was unlikely to be still around by the time someone pressed that red button to take the world off its hinges.

Russell himself gave the answer when he wrote somewhere, "It is necessary to care deeply for things which will not come to pass until long after we are gone." He disavowed the title "Christian," but it would be hard to find a more powerful example of what Paul meant by "laying a good foundation for the future." To be a man rather than a happy vegetable is to be conscious not only of a debt to the past but of a responsibility for the future as well. It is so to live in the present as to be confident that when the final shape of things is revealed, one will be able to point to a brick in that edifice and claim, "That has my name upon it!"; just as the foundations of a world freed from the threat of nuclear extinction will undoubtedly boast a cornerstone with Bertrand Russell's name across it.

According to classical theology, man's great sin is pride. Personally, I would say that the great sin of the modern world is not pride but cruelty. But just a short way behind cruelty is another besetting sin of our time—triviality. Never have such fantastic technical resources and human ingenuity been dedicated to such paltry, short-lived ends. Personal fame and public culture are rooted in nothing more durable than whims which are as changeable as the wind. Indeed, it is one justification for preaching in our time that the much maligned pulpit remains one of the few points in the modern world from which ordinary people can be confronted with serious ideas.

A strong sense of historical responsibility has given way to a lamentable feeling amongst our generation that providing things hold together for their lifetime and possibly the lifetime of their children, then that's the most they can hope for. But if there had not been men and women prepared to stand for things that could not possibly come to pass until long after they were gone, we should still be living in caves, at the mercy of the elements, our minds darkened by superstition and fear.

There is only one way man can recover the sense of his essential dignity in a trivial and trivializing society—enlist himself to causes which will not exhaust themselves before he exhausts himself. None are so pathetic as the people who have outlived the causes to which they have given their lives. Eaten away by nostalgia, they linger on with "left-over time to kill," hearing the ghostly trumpets of past battle calls in the mind, but knowing no longer in which direction to charge.

This sense of historical responsibility is one thing which Christians share with Marxists. There are many differences between us, but this at least we have in common—the sense that we have a duty to shape the future and the hope that it can be shaped in conformity to our dreams. Listen to some words of a friend of mine, James Klugman, a veteran Marxist from the early 1930s, and though he may sue me for saying it, one of the saintliest men I know:

> Communists have a belief, if you like, a *faith* in man. A faith in the capacity of men and women to change their world and in so doing, themselves to build a world where men and women as part of society can fully develop their infinitely varied human talents, can enjoy art in its every aspect, and love and affection untrammeled by cash and commerce. . . . A communist who helps bring about the advance of humanity sees himself living in those he leaves behind.[2]

[2] Klugman, *What Kind of Revolution?* (Panther Books, 1968), p. 186.

All right, so those great scourges of mankind—hunger, discrimination, and injustice—are not going to be abolished in my lifetime or even that of my children's children. But I am not going to lie down and bemoan the hopelessness of it all. I can take one short step, strike one puny blow, lay one tiny brick on behalf of the future. For that is where the citizenship of the Christian lies.

The *length* of God's love requires that we think long thoughts, wrestle with great issues though they throw us, and step back from time to time for some deep reflection on where this circus procession we call life is heading. A sense of perspective is everything: remember that a penny is big enough to blot out the sun if you hold it close enough to the eye. This is how men in their myopia manage to confuse the trivial and the profound, the evanescent and the enduring.

In his proclamation of the kingdom of God, Jesus offered men a cause which would not exhaust itself before they exhaust themselves, a vision that needs the whole stage of history to contain it, and a program which speaks not only to man's social and political concerns but also his inner spiritual needs. When men of goodwill debate the ultimate purposes of human life, the Christian offers the kingdom of God and humbly invites others to match it with a more majestic and comprehensive goal.

Thirdly, as to the depth of the love of God:
It is necessary to explore the limits of the possible in the realm of the Spirit.

Talk about the realm of the Spirit seems to cut us off from the Marxists and even from the humanists if we insist on that capital S for Spirit. But I cannot believe that the present struggle for man's humanity, in which many movements and individuals are engaged, either issues from the rigorously materialistic interpretation of life or has as its goal man's freedom to be a superior vegetable. If it does, then the sludge

79

has thrown up some men of fine-honed spirit, who appear to be inviting the next generation to jump back in and wallow.

As long ago as 1890, Engels in a letter to J. Bloch protested at the way the view of himself and Marx had been twisted to suggest a concept of man as a walking stomach:

> According to the materialist view of history, the *ultimately* determining element in history is the production and re-production of real life. More than this Marx and I have never asserted. Hence if somebody twists this into saying that the economic element is the *only* determining one, he transforms that proposition into a meaningless, abstract, senseless phrase.

That protest does not dispose of the differences between Christians and Marxists, but it does allow room for debate about the dimension of the Spirit.

Charles Peguy's famous epigram, "Everything begins in mysticism and ends in politics," is true in the sense that it is often some heavenly vision which inspires man's fight for earthly justice. But my own experience has been the precise opposite. If I dared to generalize, I would claim that more often in this life, everything begins in politics and ends in mysticism. There is a spring of creative energy which is an "outside" factor in political activity and leads men to wonder as to its source. Note that I am not preaching any dualism between the spiritual and material, the pious and the practical, but pointing to a *depth* in life from which we can draw the power to overcome that crippling medieval sin—*accidie*—sloth or spiritual torpor which tempts us to live far short of our capacities and limits.

Most people are aware of this "wild," unpredictable element in life which produces quite different results in apparently identical cases. Women often meet it in that very mundane area, the kitchen. Identical ingredients mixed according to the same recipe and cooked for the same length of time in the same oven result this time in a beautifully proportioned cake, that time in a sadly misshapen offering. There are wild horses in the human personality which cannot be tamed but can be harnessed; there is an element in life which we cannot subdue but which can be used to drive us beyond our best or lower than our naturally worst.

The Spirit dimension of life is the one that man never has or never could conquer. It is that upon which he is dependent. This sense of dependence is clearest seen in those areas of the world which technology has not yet decisively shaped or warped. For all our proud Western achievements in urbanization, transport, and communications, we still live in a much smaller world than that of the average African villager for whom the people in the next village are strangers. His world is peopled not only by the living but also by the spirits of the dead and the yet unborn, and it is a unitary world in which nature and history touch hands. The dimension of the Spirit does not lie beyond the boundaries of what can be tasted, handled, heard, and seen. It interpenetrates every aspect of his life, including the most material. And those who write all this off as dark superstition have little conception of the complexity and delicacy of the traditional African world view.

We are told that, for better or worse, the West has lost this Spirit dimension. I do not believe it for a second, and the proof is the prevalence in our society of magic, which is a degenerate form of Spirit-life—the attempt to use for our own purposes that upon which we are ultimately dependent. In the realms of money, sex, and politics, men act upon anything but scientific, rational principles: so besotted are they with a jumble of superstition, empty ritual, and primitive fears that they are in urgent need of that old gospel power of exorcism to free them from demons.

Space exploration has taught us that if there is anything in this world that man wants to do badly enough (assuming that this thing is not intrinsically absurd), sooner or later he will evolve the mechanisms by which to do it. The limits of the possible in the physical world now lie way out in the bright blue yonder. But how about that other world which inter-penetrates this one—the world of the Spirit—dare we formulate a similar rule that in *this* world too, if man wants badly enough to do something which is good and wholesome, he can lay hold of the power by which to do it? Where lie the limits of the possible in this other world?

Here the Christian faces a crucial challenge. For the church is meant to be a laboratory of the kingdom in which the promises of God are put to the test of practicability. But there is one sad difference between this laboratory of the kingdom and those which have made space travel possible. The scientist's achievements may be brilliant, but his claims are always cautious. Unless he has an almost unshakable case, he will not declare something to be so. *Our* claims are breathtaking—but our results? Granted, the Christian does not work in a material which can be measured, put under a microscope, or through a computer, but ought he not to have *some* kind of evidence that the man in the street is disposed to consider as proof that he is not deluded?

In the crusade of our time, Christians are intended to be the sappers and miners of the bright company of the socially engaged, exploring the depths of the Spirit dimension from which might come inexhaustible sinews of war when our other ammunition is used up. And we shall not be adoring the Spirit dimension for its own sake, as some mystics do, nor seeking to manipulate it for our own ends as the spiritualist does, but finding ways to use that which we cannot command and upon which we are dependent, to change the world.

I am well aware that I haven't used much theological or biblical language in stating these convictions of mine. This is because I want to take with me not only the committed but also the venturesome, who cannot make Christian affirmations but are sufficiently open-minded to explore the dimensions I have tried to describe. But I would be less than honest if I did not state roundly that for me, Jesus is the one who stands at the intersection of these dimensions and that it is through him I gain access to the truth and experience they demarcate.

As for Christians who fear a watering-down of their faith in such "secular" statements of conviction, I would plead— let's take down the fences and abandon that unthinking orthodoxy which is unconsciousness. If we really believe that Jesus is the truth, what have we to fear? Wherever we plunge into this strange, fascinating world, we will find, in the phrase of Teilhard de Chardin, that Jesus is the Omega Point—the destination to which all roads of truth lead.

CHAPTER 8

Sacrifice or Waste?

"What is the point of all your sacrifice?"
Isaiah 1:11.

That's a good question. And here is another: Why is it that sacrifice, once one of the proudest words in the language, tinkles so unmusically upon the ears of our generation?

There is a *political* reason. In 1914 men marched to war with the perfervid oratory of the patriots and politicians ringing in their ears. They were off to fight for a better world. Those who survived came back to all the old muddle and mess, greed and rapaciousness; and they lived to see their own children put on uniforms again in 1939 to reap the whirlwind sown in the aftermath of their war. So when they read down the melancholy lists of the glorious dead of two wars and remember their own fallen comrades, they ask, "What was it all *for?*" And he is a clever man who can tell them. The explanation they choose to believe, right or wrong, is that the sacrifice of ordinary people was used by the power-hungry for their own ends. So they don't intend to be caught again.

There is a *religious* reason. Many people are revolted by that strain in Christian theology and hymnology which harks back to the blood-obsessed days of the Old Testament. They can find nothing elevating or moving in references to "fountains filled with blood," and robes "washed in the blood of the Lamb." The attempt to depict the death of Jesus in terms appropriate to Old Testament sacrifice they think either meaningless or plain barbaric. And I stand with them. I cannot see that all the blood and gore add anything whatever to the meaning of Christ's death; indeed, that verse in

Hebrews 9 to the effect that "everything is cleansed by blood and without the shedding of blood there is no forgiveness" is just not true—it is denied again and again by both Christ's teaching and his actions. Blood imagery may have made sense to the first-century Jew, but it is a hindrance to the faith of twentieth-century man and has debased the coinage of sacrifice by burdening it with abhorrent overtones.

There is a *scientific* reason. Technology has shown that physical power, judiciously applied, can enrich human life, and without doubt, most forms of inconvenience and discomfort have been abolished by scientific skill. In this dynamic world, input and output, action and reaction, are so precisely related that the idea of sacrifice—investing human resource without hope of return—seems quaintly odd. In scientific terms, expenditure of *anything* without proportionate reward is not sacrifice but *waste*. The feeling that sacrifice is irrelevant may be based upon a perverted understanding of science, but it is nonetheless prevalent for that.

Is it possible to rehabilitate sacrifice as a master principle of life? Only, I suspect, if we can clear up a number of misconceptions about it.

WE MUST DISTINGUISH BETWEEN SACRIFICE AND WASTE

1. *Sacrifice as an end in itself is waste.* There is a strand in Christian tradition which equates pain with virtue—it is a strange dark world of hair shirts and scourgings—and seems to be based upon the theory that we cannot both be good and be comfortable. Only a narrow line separates this religious desire to embrace pain from the psychological perversions of masochism.

There is no virtue in pain itself. Some of those who preach most eloquently about the blessings of suffering do so from a situation of hale and hearty good health. Suffering brutalizes as many as it ennobles, and though it has been and can be

85

used creatively, it is no part of the gospel that it should be invited. Sacrifice as an end in itself is a perversion, a waste of precious human resources.

2. *Artificial sacrifice is waste.* C. S. Lewis once tartly remarked of a woman he knew, "She lives for others. And you can tell the others by their hunted look!" Some of the most irritating people on earth are those self-consciously seeking causes on behalf of which to lay their all upon the altar. They are the legions of short-lived enthusiasts, for whom life is not so much an experience as a succession of crusades. They are not satisfied to do good: they must be able to show the scars to prove it. If they are robbed of a glorious encounter with lions in the arena, they will go and seek them out in some zoo. They cannot pass a fiery furnace without wanting to jump into it or see a cross without trying to nail themselves to it. They need to be protected from their better selves and shown that what they fondly believe to be sacrifice is simply exhibitionism.

3. *Illegitimate sacrifice is waste.* Many families know the tragedy of the single woman who abandons all her own prospects in order to care for an aged parent or relative. And too many families suffer the tyranny of aged parents who use their dependence as a form of power over those children with too fine a sense of obligation. The last thing I would wish to do is deny the claims of kinship or devalue the act of those who unselfishly give up their own chances of fulfillment through a sacrifice as painful as it is sublime. Yet, beyond a certain point, the present generation has no right to sacrifice itself to the past generation. It may be right to sacrifice itself to the future generation, for that is how the drama of history is carried forward, but not to the past.

In the last resort, no one can live his life through someone else. Each one has a personal destiny and a task for the kingdom which is peculiarly his. Therefore, there are some sacrifices which we have not the right to make. Sometimes it must be sadly concluded that a magnificent act of renunciation is not sacrifice but waste.

SACRIFICE IS ALWAYS AN INITIATIVE AND NOT JUST AN ACCEPTANCE

Sacrifice must be distinguished from the heroic acceptance of the inevitable. The human quality demonstrated may be the same, but the motive is different. Sacrifice is always active, never passive. It seeks to introduce a new element into a situation; to change things. In this sense it is an initiative and never a mere acceptance. Hence, Jesus facing Jerusalem says, "I lay down my life freely. No man takes it from me!"

It might even be said that true sacrifice *always* introduces a new element into a situation, even though things seem outwardly little changed. Consider the story of the Russian Orthodox saint Elizabeth Pilenko, known as Mother Maria, as told in Victor Gollancz's *Year of Grace:*

> Mother Maria was arrested by the Gestapo and sent to the concentration camp at Ravensbruck. The story of her life is only now being pieced together. She was known even to the guards as "that wonderful Russian nun," and it is doubtful whether they had any intention of killing her. She had been there two and a half years when a new block of buildings was erected in the camp, and the prisoners were told that these were to be hot baths. A day came when a few dozen prisoners from the women's quarters were lined up outside the buildings. One girl became hysterical. Mother Maria, who had not been selected, came up to her. "Don't be frightened," she said. "Look, I will take your turn." And in line with the rest she passed through the doors.

[1] Gollancz, *A Year of Grace* (Gollancz, 1950), p. 209.

The story goes that the guards were so moved by the death of Mother Maria that for a little while the gassing of prisoners stopped. Soon, the sorry processions of prisoners were shuffling into the gas chambers again, but for a moment in time something important had happened—at the heart of chaos and brutality a blow had been struck on behalf of sanity and love. So sacrifice is always more than stoicism— the stiff-upper-lip acceptance of the worst that can come one's way. It has its origins not in man's courage but in his dignity, his determination to retain always one area of initiative, over himself, whatever else may be outside his control.

Sacrifice is often the only simple solution to complex problems. Take the problem which haunted Captain Scott and his companions as they struggled to get back from the South Pole to their base camp. One member of the team, Captain Oates, was so badly frostbitten that it was clear he would have to be carried, a task which, in their weakened state, would rob the rest of the team of any chance of reaching safety. On the other hand, it was unthinkable that Captain Oates should be abandoned by his comrades. The problem was impossibly difficult, yet Captain Oates cut through all its complexities with a solution at once beautifully simple and yet infinitely costly. He walked out into the night, removing an intolerable burden from the backs and consciences of his companions. That story provides the best working definition of sacrifice I know—the offer of simple but costly solutions to complex human problems.

SACRIFICE IS MORE THAN SELF-DENIAL: IT IS SELF-TRANSCENDENCE

Being human, we tend to deride things we have never had or have had to give up. This is a psychological dodge which enables us to live with our deprivations. But this understandable peccadillo has at times throughout Christian history turned into something much less attractive—a life-denying puritanism which waves a boney finger of anathema at all those activities of life it does not feel it right to indulge in. At root, this false austerity derives from lack of moral discrimination—wholesome things are condemned outright because they are capable of abuse. Television is evil because it may keep people from church on Sunday evenings; eating and drinking and loving must be hedged about with so many prohibitions and warnings that the life is choked out of them.

Those who impose upon themselves such feats of iron self-denial would claim that they are living a sacrificial life. In fact, the true poignancy of sacrifice lies elsewhere—in the choice not between the bad and the good, but between the good and the better. Though it may require great strength of will to sacrifice the obviously bad for the good, the choice is usually a simple one. But it takes rare sensitivity to know when the good must be offered up for the sake of the better. The missionary who accepts long separation from his family to serve in a distant land is turning his back not upon the bad for the sake of the good, but upon the good for the sake of the better. It is this quality of moral discrimination which transforms sacrifice from a negative self-denial into a positive self-transcendence.

Jesus put this truth succinctly in the parable of the pearl of great price. The merchant who sought, found, and paid for the pearl was not sacrificing the bad for the good, but the good for the better. He was not paying dirt for diamonds, but diamonds for *the* diamond. By hard work and experience, he had accumulated a collection of pearls which the average man would have been more than satisfied to own. But he was driven on by the conviction that there was to be found somewhere a better beyond the best for which he was prepared to risk losing everything. This self-transcendent quality of true sacrifice is a combination of idealism and sensitivity which inspires us to search for the best beyond the good, the truth beyond many truths, the mark beyond our

furthest aim. But without some kind of gospel, some philosophy of life whose values are backed by an authority we are
prepared to accept, sacrifice never gets beyond the point of
self-denial—a trait admirable but arid.

SACRIFICE AS MINIMAL AND MAXIMAL DEMAND

There is always a danger of sacrifice degenerating into the
Minimal Demand. The parrot-cry "People won't take that
sort of thing!" leads to a scaling-down of moral demands to
the level of the conveniently acceptable. Contemporary
church life has molded itself around the Minimal Demand—
tithing is unacceptable and so is replaced by 1 percent
giving; the ten-minute address takes the place of the full-
blown sermon because people are easily bored; the requirements of mission must be dove-tailed into the blank spaces
of crowded engagement diaries.

The philosophy of the Minimal Demand is one reason why
the older generation have forfeited the respect of the young.
We fail to make contact with them not because we make too
many demands upon them, but because we make too few, and
of the wrong kind. From one angle, the present ferment
amongst students can be seen as a reaction against the very
cosseting society has given them. Those die-hards who
fulminate against the selfishness and laziness of students
should ask themselves why it is that these same students who
want no truck with a time-serving society will, under
different circumstances, risk clashes with the police, imprisonment, and occasionally death.

Those political and ideological movements, such as
nationalism and communism, which make ultimate demands
upon people are never short of volunteers. The imperious
demand "Your soul—now and forever, in life and in death!"
is heard by many who are deaf to a request for half an hour of
their time in the cause of sporadic good works. Is it not a
strange thing about human nature that there are people who

will not give you half a crown but will respond favorably to a request for a thousand pounds? There are people who cannot squeeze half an hour out of their diaries yet will, under different conditions, give their whole lives to a cause. The philosophy of the Minimal Demand is swept aside because it is based upon a miniscule vision. It is not a call to sacrifice but for the acceptance of reasonable inconvenience; not the pouring out of lifeblood but the disposition of a surplus.

What, then, is the Maximal Demand? In one sense, it varies with the situation, but in the most fundamental sense it is a constant factor underlying all human situations. In theological terms it could be put this way. Everything we possess, including life itself, is a gift from God, and, *therefore*, any sacrifice can be seen as merely returning what has been borrowed to its rightful owner—"We give thee but thine own, whate'er the gift may be," as that offertory hymn puts it. Yes, with one exception. There is one possession over which we have absolute right of disposal, which God has no power to claim—the human will. So the psalmist characterized the supreme sacrifice as "a broken and a contrite spirit." In terms of the rules God himself has laid down, he has no right to command the human will. His sovereignty stops short at that point. Whatever the circumstances that invoke it, the right of self-disposal is the ultimate sacrifice, the only sacrifice of which man is capable that is cosmic in proportions.

This is not such a rarefied religious concept as it might at first sound. Every human problem you care to name, political, economic, social, and religious, is either caused by or exacerbated by a deep corruption of the human will. So whatever technical adjustments must be made in any of these areas to solve man's problems, the offering up of the will, voluntary acceptance of mastery by a power which is not subject to corruption, is the key to personal and social regeneration.

Now bring Jesus into the picture and it becomes clear why throughout Christian history he has been described as

91

offering up the "perfect" sacrifice. It fits each of the conditions I have described. His was a sacrifice of the will—"Not my will but thine be done!" It was an initiative and not mere acceptance of *force majeur*—"He set his face to go to Jerusalem." It was true sacrifice and not mere waste; there was no embracing of pain for its own sake—did he not pray that the cup might pass from him? And most important, it was the sacrifice of the good for the better. He exchanged the good life, of teaching, healing, and service, for the better—an act of obedience so absolute that it has changed the course of history, and makes him not merely a fond memory or a fine example but a living presence and a lively hope.

CHAPTER 9

Holy Unemployable?

"There was a man sent from God whose name was John."
John 1:6.

To state the blindingly obvious—the traditional concept of the ministry has gone into the melting pot. Two main pressures have put it there—a chronic shortage of candidates for ordination, and rediscovered theological insights about the nature of ministry as the work of the whole church. I would like to say a lot about both, but must content myself with hoping that *something* emerges from the melting pot soon, even if it is only a strong smell of burning!

Meanwhile, there is the question of *your* parson, who, whilst the debate and ferment rage about his head (and probably within it too), gets on with doing what it has been given to him to do. Statistically speaking, the chances are that he is of the old dispensation—a model produced before the theological schools began retooling to make the Mark-Two minister. It is unlikely that your parson is a complacent fool. He is aware that all is not well; probably he knows where he hurts better than the theological specialists poised anxiously over him. But every moment of his waking life he is required to respond, not to what ought to be, nor even to what he would like to be, but to what is.

So without prejudice, as the lawyers say, to this radical rethinking about ministry, I want to talk about the flesh and blood man who is your parson. What does he think he is doing? What do you think he is doing? What does God think he is doing? A convenient framework within which to examine these questions is provided by this verse in the prologue to John's Gospel—"There was a man sent from God whose name was John." This is the first reference in that profound account of creation to human agency having been entrusted by God with any part of the task.

THERE WAS A MAN

The parson is a man—and, I hasten to add, she can be a woman too! I have no desire to lend the authority of this text to quite the silliest argument in the modern church, that against the ordination of women. Some of the best men in the ministry are women, if you see what I mean! The parson is a man—a statement the average congregation will receive with the hoots of derision reserved for a fool who told them he had made the extraordinary discovery that two and two equals four. Yet people who are well aware that two and two equals four still behave as though the parson were not so much a man as a disembodied bundle of virtue they pay to be good on their behalf.

Why God chooses men to be his messengers is, I suppose, a mystery. No doubt legions of angels would convey divine truth with greater accuracy *and* cause the kind of stir advertising agencies seek to create when they want to catch the public's attention. It must have something to do with the nature of Christian truth which does not exist in a vacuum but lives through a man and gains special authenticity from having been wrung out of his doubts and uncertainties. The truth becomes incarnate within a personality to point the moral that if the messenger can make it his own, so can any man.

In the modern world, the parson needs to be a man in a special sense. During the war a notice was displayed in employment exchanges, which read: "All persons in the above age groups are required to register for national service except lunatics, the blind, and ministers of religion." A number of interesting interpretations could be placed upon that classification but the main point is clear—the ministry was a sheltered occupation; the parson's special gifts or strange work rendered him unavailable for mundane service, even in a time of national emergency. In the quarter of a century that has since elapsed, the acids of skepticism have eaten away the protective cover around the parsonic image. People no longer bring out their best china when he comes to tea, nor does a clerical collar guarantee him a railway compartment to himself. The world has lost its reverential awe of the special species of man whose dress and manner showed that he had turned his back upon its delights to follow some higher destiny.

This trend, which has saved many parsons from the worst excesses of their peculiar virtues, is to be applauded. Now, in every sense, the parson is just a man in the world of men. He must fight to get a hearing because his is only one voice amongst many in the marketplace of ideas. And because he is speaking to a society which is strong in its sense of self-sufficiency, he must match strength to strength. Those pale aesthetes, the clergymen of Jane Austen's novels, whose constituency seemed almost entirely composed of maiden ladies with the vapors, projected Jesus in terms of a fragile, effeminate saviorhood. Only his robust lordship can speak to the mood of our day.

I should add that in talking of the parson as a man in the world of men, I am not advocating that self-conscious mateyness which has clergymen appearing in all the colors of the rainbow and propping up bars to swap naughty stories with the boys. The ministry is blessed with some men who are colorful characters in their own right; who can with great effectiveness prop up bars with the boys. For the rest, back-slapping bounciness is not less unnatural than hand-wringing servility. To be a man amongst men is simply to participate in the same life substance, to claim neither special exemptions nor privileges, and to show that sharing God's ministry is the most natural thing in the world.

95

The parson is a man, but he is not universal man. He is a man of his generation, and that may not be yours. Quite possibly he has grown up and trained in a world quite foreign to your own. There are limits to his elasticity, his ability to span the generation gap—which creates more tensions in the church than all the theological wrangling. It is less than helpful to remind him how "Dear Dr. So and So" tended the flock in the 1930s, or even in the 1950s—with the clear implication that if he went and did likewise, things would take a turn for the better. The gospel Word is both historical and contemporary. It speaks of events that occurred once and for all a long time ago, and yet requires today's voices and accents to transmit it with living power. "Dear Dr. So and So" may have had the Word for the 1930s; it does not follow that he would have the Word for the 1970s. It is rarely given to a man to be prophetic in more than one time. The only authentic word any man can speak is that wrung out of his experience, and his experience has been largely molded by his generation. That word may sound jarringly unfamiliar to you, but it is wise to heed it—you may be hearing the alien accents of a Jesus for the 1970s.

Is there any need to remind you that if the parson is a man, he has a breaking point and will quite often reach it? By definition, every parson is in a job too big for him, and unless he has been given the sensitivity of a rhinoceros, he carries with him always an awareness of this fact. Ordination—the laying on of hands—is not the spiritual equivalent of that operation in which a hot wire is drawn across the brain to turn a manic depressive into a happy little chappie. The parson has no God-given dispensation from doubt, frustration, and despair. Like Shylock's Jew, he bleeds when cut and cracks when intolerable burdens are laid upon him. And to draw attention to this elementary truth is not to engage in self-justification. It is common sense. After all, people who hope to get good mileage out of a car and so avoid being let down in awkward places, treat it kindly.

Of course you know all this! But the acid test of whether the point has really been taken comes when you observe a parson saying or doing something which would be normal for anyone else and are tempted to say, "I didn't expect a minister to do that!" Why ever not? Haven't we agreed he is a man? If a parson has to amputate part of his personality or twist it into unnatural shapes in order to fit some mold the church provides for him, then he is paying too big a price for his job. And more important, God is being disobeyed. It was his idea to choose *men*.

SENT FROM GOD

Implicit in the idea of being "sent" is the recognition that someone comes from *outside*. In one sense, the parson is always an alien; he comes into a situation from outside, and then sooner or later tears up his roots and moves on elsewhere. Leaving aside those abrasive encounters between parson and people that are brought to an end with sighs of relief all round, it is painful for most congregations to adjust to the challenge of an unfamiliar figure in the pulpit, a fresh voice, and different ways of doing things. Painful but necessary. The semi-nomadic life of the parson proclaims the central biblical truth that our salvation always comes to us from outside ourselves.

The means by which any people's salvation is accomplished is meant to shatter all their illusions of self-sufficiency. For saving truth does not well up from some spring in their midst, nor does it dawn upon their minds as a kind of universal apperception. It must be brought to them. It breaks in from outside. Isn't this what incarnation means? The tabernacle of God may dwell with men, but it hasn't always been so. There had to be a point when history was cloven in two; when God decisively intervened. When Charles Williams wrote his interpretation of church history,

97

The Descent of the Dove, he took heaven as the starting point of the Christian drama, claiming that though Pentecost was the visible origin of the church, its true beginning was strictly outside time.

This is the way it always is. Our salvation comes to us from outside. In the realm of human relationships, it takes someone else to break into our prisons of self-preoccupation and release us—there is no lock on the inside of the cell door. No one ever thought his way through to Christ by cunning mental application. Someone had to tell him, or better, show him.

So this clerical wanderer on the face of the earth is, however inadequate he may be, a concrete reminder to any group of people that there may be many things they can do for themselves, but they cannot save themselves. When next, therefore, you are tempted to moan that the new parson is cutting across long-established ways of doing things, you might turn your complaint into a parable, and see him not just as a square peg in a round hole but the outsider in your midst who points to that other Outsider waiting to break in with the gift of salvation.

That a man should be "sent from God" speaks also of the nature of the parson's call to the ministry. And what holy hokum is talked on this subject in some quarters! There are parsons whose sense of conviction that they were intended for the ministry was borne in upon them as clearly as though someone had tapped them on the shoulder and spoken in their ear, and that conviction has never wavered or diminished for a moment. There are others who have appeared before boards of examiners almost incoherent in their effort to make sense of a bewildering welter of ideas and impressions too vague to be rationalized into some Damascus Road experience. The best they could do was to throw themselves upon the church's mercy and accept its judgment about the validity of their call. Both groups have produced some great ministers.

I confess here to a purely personal prejudice. When I had some responsibility in the United Church of Zambia for helping to select ministerial candidates, I viewed with acute suspicion those who affirmed that God had called them at the age of four and that by the time they were five, they were standing on stools in the nursery, preaching their early sermons. But even here one's judgment can be confounded. F. A. Iremonger describes the infant William Temple in the nursery: As a child he had his own robe-case, at the top of which was laid a carefully folded surplice and a diminutive miter. Robed in these, he would give out a hymn and preach—usually about conduct—to the nursery maid and any others who might be interested.[1] William Temple was clearly a law unto himself. Yet it is significant that in spite of his early leanings toward the ministry, his eventual road was a serpentine one, along which he agonized every step of the way. So it is still fairly safe to claim that God rarely calls boys to do the work of men. If the Bible is any guide, he seems to prefer tentmakers and vinedressers and fishermen with gnarled hands to fresh-faced youths.

If we add any self-insight we possess to what the psychologists have taught us about human nature, it is clear that our motives for doing *anything* are mixed. Within us, ambition wars with humility, power-hunger with the desire for goodness. It is a man of rare single-mindedness, or an extremely simple one, who can say, "For this reason, and this reason alone, I did such a thing!" Hence, it is often only in retrospect that a man can see his call to the ministry was a true one, and even then he will wonder at the strange paths his life has taken. On looking back, he may be fairly confident that he is now where he was intended to be—but what a close thing it was!

There is something to be said for the apparently callous advice the more hard-bitten minister is prone to give any

[1] Iremonger, *William Temple* (O.U.P., 1948), p. 7.

prospective candidate who seeks his counsel—If you *can* stay out, then *do!* And the temper of our time aids the process of unnatural selection. The financial rewards of the ministry are derisory and its social status definitely diminished, and there are a thousand and one worthwhile jobs a man can do to serve humanity; so the modern candidate for the ministry is likely either to be possessed of an intense conviction or to have a screw loose—two conditions fairly easily distinguishable!

The idea of being "sent from God" also raises the question of the minister's authority. There was a time when this authority was beyond question. Behind the parson's lightest word was thrown all the weight of an infallible church and an inerrant Bible. At the present time, though there are those amongst his hearers who will be inclined to believe him when he states that something is so because the Bible or the church or the creeds say it is, there are many more who will be moved only by the self-evident truth of what he says. If they believe at all, it will be because what is true for him hits the mark as being true for them also. One could quote Paul to the effect that there is an inner witness in every man which testifies to the truth of the gospel, but it is very dangerous for lazy men to rely upon supernatural help in transforming pious clichés into words winged with fire.

We live in a time when the minister is required to lay his integrity on the line with absolute openness. He cannot hide behind the skirts of the bishops or the robes of the doctors. He cannot pick other men's flowers, preach other men's sermons, or recite other men's beliefs with any hope of carrying conviction. Because all establishments are suspect and a deep rebelliousness is stirring within the spirit of man, the authority of the parson is acutely personal. He has not been sent from God with any message. He *is* the message—its weight is his weight, and its convincing power is a direct function of his spiritual and intellectual capacity to open himself to the gospel. Men who skip along the surface of life, dallying with ideas, can neither know nor tell of the depths of Christ. And those whose credo is a thing of scissors and paste—snippets of biblical and theological gossip stuck together in some sort of shape—will succeed only in fabricating a cardboard Jesus, destined to be blown away by the lightest breath of the detractors.

However, to leave matters there is to be guilty of a half-truth. Though the minister's authority is personal, it has still to be conferred upon him by the people. And it is an irrevocable gift. Once the people have given a man the authority to be a minister, they cannot take that authority back if he ceases to please them. They have freed him from any groveling subservience to their every whim and fancy. His is servanthood without servility. Far from conferring upon him a patronage which he holds at their will and pleasure, the people have given the minister the power to stand against them. When Paul is before Agrippa, describing his conversion, he claims that God said to him on the Damascus Road, "Stand on your feet, for I will make you a minister, *delivering you from the people!*" This is sometimes the minister's greatest need—to be delivered from the people, who may smother him with kindness and so trap him in a silken web of obligation that it seems the basest ingratitude and treachery to stand against them with a word that cuts like a sword through the harmony and happy fellowship.

The reason why he dare stand against the people at all is that at his ordination, when the words "Take thou authority to be a minister in the church of God!" were said over him, it was not a list of church members that was thrust into his hands, but a Bible. Both he and his people stand under the Word of God, so provided his position on any issue is truly scriptural, his authority is unshakable. This, of course, is not the same thing as saying that he is bound to win every argument, nor does it guarantee him any job security when he is at odds with his people, but it is a source of strength when he has to withstand a tide of feeling flowing strongly against him.

Many elements make up the minister's sense of call, not all of which can be clearly identified. And it is a rare minister whose sense of call is not at times muted or even totally drowned. Indeed, given the present ferment in the church, any minister who has not been driven to radical self-questioning about what he is doing, and why, is almost certainly out of touch with reality—he typifies that popular parody of Kipling, "If you can keep your head when all about you are losing theirs—you just don't understand the problem!" In times of corrosive doubt and loneliness, the minister has precious little to hang on to other than those words of Jesus, "You have not chosen me. I have chosen you"—and this must pass for certainty.

WHOSE NAME WAS JOHN

At the very heart of this tremendous theological statement about creation in John's Gospel, one suddenly stumbles across an oddly human touch—reference to a man's name, John. It seems quite out of place. Every other link in this majestic argument is a phrase throbbing with unearthly power, "In the beginning was the Word," "The Word was with God," "All things were made by him," "In him was life and the life was the light of men," and then—". . . a man sent from God, whose name was John." Obviously, if there was a point at which the whole operation might break down, it is this one. For "John" is not a cipher for invincible power; it identifies a weak, fallible human being. John is vulnerable and dependent.

So too, the minister is vulnerable and dependent. And he can hardly complain that no one warned him in advance that this must be his destiny. Didn't Paul tell the Corinthians that those who followed Jesus would become a *theatron*—a public spectacle like the hapless animals led into the arena to be slaughtered for entertainment of the crowd? "We are treated," he said, "as the scum of the earth, the dregs of humanity, to this very day." Thus, if the minister is in any sense God's representative, then in his vulnerability and dependence he represents not God's power but his powerlessness.

Christianity shares many truths with other religions, but in one regard at least it is unique—in testifying to a God who puts himself at the mercy of men. Where other faiths speak proudly of man's need of God, Christianity speaks strangely of God's need of man. Was this not historically true of Jesus? He needed a womb to carry him and a human breast at which to suck. He needed a father to shield him from Herod's wrath, and friends to share his mission. He needed someone to help carry his cross, and he needed someone to roll away the stone from his tomb. The vulnerability of Jesus is the vulnerability of God who, in a reversal of all human experience, strengthens by his weakness and enables by his impotence.

Like God at the mercy of men, the minister is at the mercy of his people. He is dependent upon them, not merely for the sinews of life, but also for the support and forbearance to sustain his ministry. A long time ago, P. T. Forsyth wrote, "Earnest ministers suffer more from the smallness of their people than from their sins, and far more than from their unkindness. Our public may kill by its triviality a soul which could easily resist the assaults of oppression or wickedness." [2] Who ministers to the minister? At one level, I suppose, it is the bishop or superintendent who is *pastor pastorum*, but in the intimate commerce of his life, it is the people who have it within their power to make his ministry a radiant testimony or a living hell.

I have a theory that in the end of the day a congregation gets the minister it deserves. And this, not because the invitation system is infallible, but because sensitive lay folk can reinforce a minister where he is weakest and multiply his

[2] Quoted by Jenkins, *The Gift of Ministry* (Faber, 1947), p. 148.

strengths. No amount of lay support can turn a sow's ear into a silk purse—a Joe Bloggs into an Alexander Whyte—but it can make the difference between fulfillment and failure. The least gifted of ministers have exercised a powerful influence because their people sustained them; men of towering ability have come crashing because the insensitivity and hostility of their congregations were leaden weights about their feet. So pervasive is this mutuality that when a person must be accounted a failure, his people would be wise to ask, not "Where did he go wrong?" but "Where did we let him down?"

Just as the powerlessness of God embodies his judgment, so the minister's dependence also confronts his people with a kind of judgment. We cannot project ourselves backwards historically to find out whether, faced with the powerlessness of God in Jesus, we would have responded any differently from those first-century Jews; the nearest we can get to an answer is to note our reaction to those most dependent upon us. In the context of the Christian community, the minister is the utterly dependent one. When a child is given a name at baptism, that name—John—symbolizes a solemn obligation on the church's part to cherish, support and strengthen him. The minister, too, has a name, and a soul to be saved. Many a ministerial soul has been lost in churches which practice a grotesque parody of Protestantism and believe in the priesthood of all believers except the parson.

The modern world is ruled more by economics than theology. So let's summarize the issue in those terms. Take a close look at what the minister, any minister, does and gives, and ask yourself coldly, "Where else could we get such value for under a thousand quid a year?"

CHAPTER 10

Saved by Cosmic Man

"The first Adam became a living soul; whereas the last Adam has become a life-giving spirit." I Corinthians 15:45.

In thousands of pulpits this Good Friday, preachers will be grappling with the meaning of the death of Jesus. And because this was one of the most mysterious events of history, all kinds of theories will be put forward to explain it.

Some preachers will chill their congregations' blood with graphic descriptions of the physical agony of Jesus, the thirst, the stretching, the heat. Nothing will be spared, not one drop of blood nor a single wince of pain—in exquisite detail the physiology of crucifixion will be reported and the feelings of good folk lacerated by the suggestion that in some strange way the very intensity of Jesus' suffering has helped to save them. It will be claimed, without foundation, that Jesus suffered as no man before him or since has suffered. In fact, there are modern refinements of torture which make crucifixion seem merciful in contrast. Jesus was at least allowed to die a man. Some exponents of the part of pain deny their victims even that dignity and reduce them to howling animals. We are not saved by pain; not even by the pain of Jesus.

Other preachers will be preoccupied with strange trans-actions purported to have taken place within God's being. Congregations will be taken to the law courts and the slaughterhouse and invited to consider theories which are an insult both to human intelligence and God's nature. Human parents, for example, who are not unaccustomed to dealing with wayward children, will be asked to believe that God the Father finds it impossible to forgive a guilty child without first punishing an innocent one. With terms such as *propitiation*, *expiation*, *satisfaction*, and *ransom* exploding around their bewildered heads, some Christians must secretly wonder whether the preacher can be talking about the same God as the one of whom Jesus spoke and in whom he trusted.

All preaching of the cross is not of this kind, thank God, but there is enough of it around to make Good Friday a trial to Christians who do not find sickly sentimentality or dark legalism much help in trying to understand the meaning of Jesus' death.

So let's start with what we know to be a simple historical fact. A man died. And because that man was Jesus, we must consider the meaning of his death at three levels, in ascending order of importance. The first two I shall mention briefly; it is with the third that I am chiefly concerned.

A MAN DIED—AND MANKIND WAS IMPOVERISHED

At the most elementary level of understanding, a man died, and had not the church kept him in remembrance, his loss would hardly have been noticed. An anonymous Middle Eastern peasant would have met his end like thousands of others, in total obscurity. Jesus could have been any man; he *was* Everyman in the sense that his death symbolizes all the rest—the uncounted legions of those whose loss is unmarked beyond some private circle of grief.

Our sense of the enormity of death has been dulled by the horrendous events of the twentieth century. When the *Titanic* sank in 1912 with the loss of 1,500 lives, the world was shaken for months. In 1916, when 60,000 men perished in the mud of the Somme in a few hours, Britain was aghast for days. But by the end of the World War II, the human mind, in sheer self-defense, had grown a protective shell against mounting horror, and the revelation that over six million Jews had been wiped off the face of the earth at Mauthausen, Auschwitz, and Treblinka was received with numb acceptance. It is only a short step from incomprehension to indifference: the statistics of death, from hunger, war, disease, and road accidents, begin to bounce off us; we shake our heads sadly and pass on our way.

Possibly it was to combat this growing insensitivity to the obscenity of death that the body of an unknown British soldier was disinterred from the battlefields of the Western Front and buried amongst kings in Westminster Abbey in 1920. The Unknown Warrior represents 800,000 comrades who lie in unmarked graves, and his very anonymity has become the mark of signal honor. With an effort that grows more labored as time goes by, the British public tries, for a few moments each year, to focus its attention upon one death which stands for all the rest; to bend its mind round the truth that anyone who dies is *somebody*—a loss not merely to a handful of relatives and friends, but to all mankind.

So it is well that the church enacts each year this ritual commemoration of the death of Jesus—one death which stands for all the rest. Any death, however obscure, is an irreparable loss to humanity—that precise combination of qualities, that particular balance of strengths and weaknesses, can never be duplicated. In the industrial world, men whose promotion depends upon the removal of their seniors, either through retirement or death, are said to be "waiting for dead man's shoes," but there is a sense in which none of the living can step into a dead man's shoes—they never quite fit because they were made for a unique human being.

Every death, whether of Jesus Bar-Joseph of Nazareth or Joe Bloggs of Birmingham, impoverishes mankind, and unless we are sensitive to this fact, we end up by devaluing the living. Confine our ritual mourning to the passing of the great and the mighty and we are already on the road to an elitist society which can spawn such obscenities as Nazism. Good Friday commemorates the death of a particular man, but it also gives us an opportunity of remembering all the rest. We may have lost most by the passing of Jesus, but mankind loses something by every passing.

A TRUE MAN DIED—AND MANKIND WAS JUDGED

The events of Holy Week prove conclusively that human society cannot tolerate the true man, the one totally obedient to the law of his being. His goodness bursts out of our religious systems, his sense of justice cannot be accommodated within our political structures, and our social networks are torn apart by the intensity of his love. We can cope with the "grays" of human nature, the products of compromise and conformity, but we cannot come to terms with the "blacks" and the "whites"—which is why Judas ends up at the end of a rope and Jesus on a gibbet.

Those systems which man creates to help him solve the basic problems of existence sooner or later assume a new role in his life, becoming so demanding that they imprison that which they were intended to cherish—his spirit. In human affairs, the point is always reached where, in Emerson's words, "things are in the saddle, and ride mankind." It is a symptom of man's egotism that he must invest whatever he is dependent upon with the qualities of divinity. So the state becomes a God, the institutional church an inerrant high priest, and the family, even, an obsession. And the sentiments these absolute systems evoke—political obedience, religious loyalty, family solidarity—are judged to be essential to a man's fulfillment.

But what happens when a man arrives on the scene with an exact sense of priorities; who will give absolute obedience to God and only conditional loyalty to any human system? Jesus was neither the first nor the last man in history to find himself in this predicament, but he is the classic case of one whom the systems conspire to destroy because they cannot contain him. The thousand half-truths by which we are content to live rise up to choke out the whole truth which judges them.

I once had a Yorkshire landlady who prided herself on the whiteness of her sheets. And sure enough, when the lines of washing flapped gaily in the breeze on a Monday morning, her sheets shone dazzling white—an effect not hindered by the fact that the dirty gray pit slag heap provided a suitably somber background. But one day it snowed, the slag heap acquired a sparkling white topcoat, and my landlady's sheets against *that* background seemed slightly less resplendent. This, says John, is the nature of judgment: light has come into the world and men prefer darkness—or at least that half-light in which the shabbiest garment seems radiant and the most dubious qualities command uncritical admiration. Then one enters who fulfills the role of Lucifer—the Bringer of Light—and those who love darkness rise up to destroy the Killer of the Dream. That reference in Revelation to Jesus as "the bright star of dawn" is not without its note of menace—it symbolizes the moment the game is up for a world which delights to live in shadows.

So the very best products of human ingenuity, the finest flower of worldly systems—Roman law and Jewish religion—are not equal to the measure of the true man, and so what they cannot dominate, they must destroy. But by that very act they are judged. Pilate condemns Jesus, but it is Roman imperialism which suffers the judgment. Annas and Caiaphas cast Jesus out as a blasphemer, but it is Jewish religion which is exposed as godless. The death of the true man is mankind's moment of judgment; its history is cursed, and its systems shatter in their inadequacy.

COSMIC MAN DIED—AND MANKIND WAS SAVED

We are greatly indebted to Teilhard de Chardin for elaborating the Pauline concept of the summing up of all things in Christ. In essence, Christianity, he writes, "is the belief in the unification of the world in God by the Incarnation." For him, Christ is the Omega Point, the crown and seal of the evolutionary process. The great upward drive of all life, from the simplest to the most complex of all organisms, does not end with man, but with the Christ-man. With the appearance of man, evolution takes a new turn—the next phase of development is not physical but spiritual, not inevitable but voluntary, not external but internal. Because of his unparalleled openness to the claims of God and his fellowmen, through spiritual insight and discipline of the will, Jesus took mankind a stage farther on its journey to unity with the source of all life. He was Cosmic Man, the second Adam, the firstborn of many brethren—the one who gathered and subdued all life in order to present it to God. That is how Paul put it— "For though everything belongs to you—Paul, Apollos, and Cephas, the world, life, and death, the present and the future, all of them belong to you, yet you belong to Christ, and Christ to God." Jesus was "The Christ" because he embodied all God's hopes for mankind in the quality of his obedience. That affirmation, "I and the Father are one," is not to be taken as the basis of a trinitarian formula—Jesus was speaking of an identity of *wills* not of *being*.

The Cosmic Man, Jesus, was the source of such elemental life power and so towered over those who encountered him that it did not seem extravagant talk to call him "the Son of God." But the key question is this. What happens when Cosmic Man dies, when the crown of the evolutionary process bites the dust? What can this mean to God, to nature, and to mankind?

There are three significant details in Matthew's account of the crucifixion (Chapter 27) which tend either to be ignored or dismissed as part of the dramatic embroidery of the story:

"Darkness fell over the whole land." (v. 45)

"The veil of the Temple was torn from top to bottom." (v. 51)

"There was an earthquake, rocks split, graves opened and gave up their dead." (v. 52)

Paul Tillich has warned us against seeking natural explanations for these strange happenings.[1] We miss the point if we waste time trying to dredge up evidence that on the day of crucifixion there was a fortuitous eclipse of the sun or a volcanic tremor which tore a graveyard apart. These elements in the story may be strictly "mythical"—in the sense that they convey some ultimate truth which lies deeper than literal fact—nevertheless they are vitally important. They show us the extent to which the death of Jesus did violence to the senses of those who witnessed it; the dread, the awe, the portentousness. And from the very garishness of the detail, we can reconstruct what the death of Jesus meant to these observers—the shattering of their conventional patterns of thought, the sense of loss and outrage which they felt nature itself shared. Taken together, these details speak of nature in uproar at the death of Cosmic Man; separately, they describe the consequences of that death.

THE SUN VEILED ITS FACE

For natural man, the sun represents the ultimate power of the universe and the source of all life. It has always reigned supreme amongst all the Gods man has worshiped and feared throughout history, for human imagination found it impossible to conceive of a greater concentration of energy or one that exercised so absolutely the power of life and death. But at the moment of Jesus' death, the sun veiled its face to acknowledge that its ultimate power had been broken for ever. Cosmic Man's unbroken sense of unity with what is greater than the sun released those who identify with him

[1] Tillich, *The New Being* (Scribner's, 1955), p. 176.

111

from slavery to any power less absolute than *his* God. Francis of Assisi got the point; in his great hymn he wrote: "Thou burning sun with golden beam, Thou silver moon with softened gleam, O praise Him!" The sun had ceased to be man's master and become his brother and fellow worshiper.

The sun remains the greatest of all natural powers, compared to which man's contrived explosions are as feeble as the flicker of a match in the beam of a searchlight. But the veiling of the sun's face was a salute to man, who having his origins in the world of nature and sharing the upward struggle of all creatures could now transcend the realm of nature and enter the realm of grace. It was a farewell wave to one who had gone beyond the limits which nature imposes on all other forms of life. Jesus in the course of his ministry gave many hints of this mastery of nature by walking on water, raising Lazarus from the dead, feeding the five thousand, and through acts of healing to correct nature's errors. Now the sun openly acknowledged what had been barely glimpsed before. As Paul puts it, the first Adam was a living soul, dependent like the rest of creation upon the sun for his existence; the second Adam was a *life-giving* spirit—a power source on his own account. Those "alive with his life" are not conditioned by the rising and setting of the sun, by heat and cold, by flood and drought, but by grace—a new form of power driving through and beyond all natural powers.

THE CURTAIN OF THE TEMPLE WAS TORN IN TWO

The space behind the temple curtain was unoccupied, originally to show that the Jews would have no truck with any form of idolatry. When Jesus died, that empty space took on a new significance. It symbolized the vacuum at the heart of Jewish religion, long hidden, now open to the light of day. Men could no longer conceal from themselves the truth that their faith had lost its saving power. All the law and the prophets, the glorious history, the observance and ceremonial, had failed to remove the scales from their eyes. They did not see that the things belonging to their peace were embodied in Jesus. The bridegroom came, and they were not awake. The messianic secret which, like an apple, because it was not plucked when ripe, would now rot and become pestilential.

But God's purposes for mankind could not be frustrated by the failure of the Jews. The rending of the temple veil proclaimed the end of God's preoccupation with one people. Cosmic Man did not die a Jew or even a Christian; he died a man. And in dying as a public spectacle, he rendered obsolete all concepts of religion based upon sacred activities called spiritual. It is as man that anyone is saved, not as Jew or believer or priest; and he can be saved where he stands, in the midst of life; he need not fight his way to some special sanctuary. Salvation for all—that is the message of the rending of the temple veil—a royal road to God opened up for every man.

Yet there is not only a promise to be grasped but a warning to be heeded in this torn curtain. Because we *will* systematize faith, institutionalize mercy, and ritualize grace, the torn veil like the shattered tomb reminds us that Jesus stands over, as well as in, every religious system, both judging and renewing it. Throughout Christian history, men have tried to repair the curtain of the temple, often misguidedly to protect the one for whose sake it was torn in the first place. But it cannot be done. Nothing and no one has any longer the right to stand between man and his destiny—which is to become part of a new creation in and through Christ.

THE GRAVES GIVE UP THEIR DEAD

This terrestrial upheaval which thrusts back into the world of men those who have been laid to rest in the earth symbolizes the truth that because of the death of Jesus, the old law of death out of birth has been revoked; a new law rules, that of life out of death. So there is foreshadowed the answer to a

113

question which has tormented men for centuries—what is there that lasts? Can anyone face the vast changefulness of the universe with any confidence that there is permanence somewhere within it? If nations rise, have their day, and vanish, and even stars fade into burnt-out cinders, what chance of survival has man, whose spirit is as impermanent as a flickering candle flame?

If there is *anything* that lasts in the universe, elementary observation suggests that it is omnipotent matter which hurtles on its endless course whilst the finest aspects of life, those expressive of love, beauty, and character, are snuffed out with indecent haste. Mountains stand majestic and immobile forever, whilst on their slopes men are born, live, and die. The universe apparently hangs on to the lowest—matter—and lets the highest—the human spirit—go. Is there about God the insanity of a man who, finding a burning house in which a child is trapped, dashes in and emerges with his hands full of trinkets, having left the child to its fate? That is what hanging on to the lowest and letting the highest go really means. It is this suspicion of divine irresponsibility which turns men into shoulder-shrugging fatalists. Harry E. Fosdick contrasts the common inscription on ancient Roman tombs—*Non fui, fui, non sum, non curo:* I was not, I was, I am not, I do not care—with the grave of Dean Alford in Canterbury, on which are inscribed the words "The inn of a traveler on his road to Jerusalem."

What made Dean Alford so certain that his last breath would not signal the end of his journey? Such assurance could only come from personal encounter with one who is living proof that the universe is not insane; that God did not allow the highest—Cosmic Man—to slip from his grasp. When Jesus committed his spirit into the Father's hands, he put it beyond death's reach. And the graves gave up their dead as though to concede that the lowest—the earth—could not hold down the highest—the human spirit. This strange dress

114

rehearsal for the resurrection was necessary to show that Cosmic Man had drunk the cup of death to the dregs, and by his death proclaimed a new law that out of death issues life for those who entrust their spirit into the Father's keeping. The crucifixion proclaimed this law: the resurrection demonstrated it.

So what need is there for morbidity on Good Friday? Why the mourning and the gloom? Possibly they are permissible on aesthetic grounds to throw the light and joy of Easter Day into great relief, but they are not permissible on theological grounds. The death of Cosmic Man transformed a natural catastrophe into an eternal triumph. "The last Adam became a life-giving spirit"—mediating a power greater than the sun, universal in availability and deathless in quality. Universal salvation, in fact. What is morbid about that?

CHAPTER 11

The Tensions of Ministry

The ordained minister owes it to his people to attempt to explain why his role in the church is the subject of such self-questioning and confusion at the present time. And the point I am anxious to get across to you in this sermon is that when due weight has been given to those of the parson's problems which are of his own making—through loss of nerve, doubt, disobedience, and frustration—there remains at the heart of the pastoral office a basic ambiguity which reflects the ambiguities of history.

Thus, the key to what is loosely called the crisis in the ministry is right outside the realm of problems and solutions. One can only make sense of it by thinking in terms of paradox, by attempting to harmonize a series of apparent contradictions. For better or for worse, it is the vocation of the ordained minister to live with and attempt to use creatively a series of built-in tensions within the pastoral office which can never be fully resolved.

The truth that the pastoral office is structured in paradox was brought home to me as I tried to wrestle with apparent inconsistencies in the testimony of two prophets of our time, Bonhoeffer and John Robinson, the former Bishop of Woolwich. In his *Letters and Papers from Prison*, Bonhoeffer urges us to live as though God does not exist, and yet on the evidence of those same letters, he spent much of his own time as a good devout Lutheran, saying his prayers, singing hymns, and preparing sermons. Surely he could not mean that *we* must live as though God does not exist, but as for him, *he* had better keep his options open?

Similarly, all the while John Robinson the prophet was arguing that the structures of Christianity must go into the melting pot, as Bishop of Woolwich he spent his days in that most traditional of pastoral offices, preaching, confirming, and ordaining. Dr. Robinson is too shrewd not to realize that his acceptance of high office did more to bolster the traditional structure of Christianity than any amount of literary fulmination is likely to undermine.

Now I do not see such apparent inconsistencies as evidence of lack of integrity in the witness of these modern servants of Christ, but as demonstrations of the truth about paradoxes in the pastoral office which neither formula nor theology can resolve. And some who claim to have purged the pastoral office of its ambiguity and apparent irrelevance have, in fact, done so by cutting the gordian knot and releasing the tensions by embracing one half of a paradox at the expense of the other. This is the way of false clarity—of greater intelligibility and sharper witness possibly—but it is not the way of the ministry. It is implicit in our ordination that we must live with these tensions without attempting to rationalize or oversimplify them. By all means we should ensure that we have isolated the *right* tensions and rid the paradoxes of any obscurities due to sloppy thinking. But when we have completed this process of stripping down, the tensions stand out all the sharper.

Let me illustrate my point by describing four of these areas of tension.

1. *The Tensions of Obedience*

This area of tension could be roughly described as the apparently contradictory role of the prophet and the priest. Not the tension, note, between the prophets and the priests in the ministry—that is a squabble with an honorable ancestry stretching back to Moses and Aaron—but the tension between prophet and priest in every minister.

117

The minister is servant of a historical word in the sense that it refers to unrepeatable events concerned with a life and work which is complete and sealed, and it is the priestly role to preserve the record of those events and rehearse them within the church forever. But this word is also an apostolic word which needs new voices and accents to tell it forth in every time as God's response to the questions the age formulates. And this is a prophetic function.

In Old Testament times, the currents of thought generated by prophet and priest sometimes converge, diverge, run parallel, or more often collide. Priestly obedience is to a tradition which enshrines what God has done, a distinctive testimony for the ages. The prophetic obedience is to a vision—of the shape of God's being reflected in the events of time. The prophet has a clear duty to urge the people forward into the unknown. The priest has an equally plain duty to preserve the people from taking an irretrievable step. The priest names the name of Jesus who is forever the Christ, Lord and Savior. The prophet takes his stand by the Jesus who is known within history by many names or none—the Jesus whose new name in Africa is Freedom, or in Asia, Bread, or in Europe, Unity.

I am well aware that I am overstating the degree of conflict in order to sharpen the argument. But if the tension between priest and prophet was acute in biblical times, how much more crucial does it become in the modern church, where the same man must discharge both prophetic and priestly functions?

Certainly there are areas of response in which there need be no conflict between prophetic and priestly obedience—where they can be harmonized—in the renewed emphasis upon the unity of worship and mission or that sacramental theology which sees the prophetic breaking in of the world upon the very heart of what used to be regarded as the most priestly of rites.

But there *are* areas of conflict and the attempt to do justice to both priestly and prophetic roles can tear a minister apart. Of this I can speak with the authority of painful experience. In my attempts to speak prophetically within a situation of racial and political conflict, I have had to live with the consequent damage done to the church and see the eroding away of my priestly authority (in the best sense of that word). For many Christians cannot live creatively with this particular tension—which is one reason why they are not in the ministry. They find it difficult to receive both challenge and comfort from the same man. That is a fact of human nature. Strike them down at the root of their deepest-held prejudices and fears, and they tend to resist your efforts to build them up in the faith. Pierce their eardrums with your prophetic thunderings, and you often render them deaf to your priestly admonition!

Because this tension is a punishing one, we succumb to the temptation to resolve it by compartmentalizing our ministry— Real Presence at the table and Vietnam in the pulpit without any theological framework of reference to relate the two. Or else we categorize ourselves as the prophets or priests of the ministry and hope at least to score 50 percent of the marks by doing one half of the job well. But there is no possibility of a creative ministry within the modern world in any such dichotomy. We can speak a truly contemporaneous, prophetic word only when the full burden of the historical truth of the gospel has rested upon us, otherwise we degenerate into commentators upon current affairs. And from being priests we become antiquarians unless that faith once delivered to the saints, of which we are guardians, is constantly exposed to that gospel which the world preaches to the church.

Should we confine ourselves exclusively to our priestly role, the people are not led forward into that thick darkness where God is. Confine ourselves to the prophetic role and there is no way of preventing the people from taking the irretrievable step into grotesque error.

There are men amongst us who feel so deeply the desire to be unambiguously prophetic that they wish to be free of priestly obligation. So be it. They will do great things for God. But not as ministers. And many of our attempts to accommodate them by stretching the meaning of ordination to take them in are a disservice to them, in restricting their freedom to be prophetic laymen, and to ourselves in obscuring the true nature of this creative tension between our prophetic and priestly roles.

2. The Tensions of Power

This particular paradox could well be described as trying to live with both the absurdity of success and the dignity of defeat.

We are followers of one who, according to Scripture, was despised and rejected of men, and we have no right to expect any different fate. We fulfill ourselves by sharing the suffering of God. We glory in the uniqueness of a faith which proclaims that God puts himself at our mercy and gives men strength through his weakness and power by his impotence. We serve the God who is content to be the anonymous neighbor, having no form or likeness that we should desire him. We know that like him we are only vindicated by defeat. *But* . . . here is the problem. . . .

We are human, with aptitudes and abilities, good in themselves, given to us by God. It is a reflection of the dignity of our creation, a consequence of having been given dominion, that what we do, we want to do well; that what we put our hands to, we strive to do with all our might. That is laudable and scriptural. As with all else, we want to make a good job of commending our Savior—to be effective and powerful servants of the word. We strain to make a success of proclaiming the divine failure. We wish to excel at pointing men to cosmic defeat.

In other words, we are trapped within a vicious circle. Our honest workmanship and legitimate skill in commending the gospel is taken up by the world, transmuted into its own coinage—from effectiveness to success—and rung up on the cash register of public acclaim. So the humble followers of a humiliated Lord emerge as T.V. personalities and public names. We are sought after for our wit or fluency or daring. In a modern world, starved of heroes, the church must render its quota for service in the public arena—no panel discussion without its outspoken cleric; no honors list without ecclesiastical representation. So hearty is the world's approbation of our successful men because they communicate in such masterly fashion that no one hears what they are saying, which is that their public stature is the very antithesis of the way salvation comes to the universe and good is wrought.

Of course, our command of modern communication and public affairs can and is used for Christ's sake. We multiply our audience by millions. We gain a mass hearing and become forces to be reckoned with. But we can never be quite comfortable. For we are haunted by this gaunt figure who mocks our eminence by his obscurity, our eloquence by his silence, our panoply by his nakedness.

It is surely one of the quainter charms of the Methodist Church, which has not yet been completely baptized into the class structure, that our dignitaries never look quite comfortable in their regalia. There is a slight air of apology about them as though conscious that someone might accuse them of having fulfilled one half of the Covenant Service affirmation— "as having all things"—to the exclusion of the other—"as having nothing"! It is to their credit that the mantle of ecclesiastical princeship does not sit easily upon their shoulders. And their unease underlines this tension in vocation which cannot be resolved. Outstanding advocacy of the gospel will result in lionization, if not from the world then from a religious constituency which delights to see and hear its star performers. For in a day when the church takes many blows, our people demand their heroes in order to bolster their confidence that we are still in business. Hence, the slogan of the second Graham Earl's Court Campaign, "Billy's Back!" is the retort of a hero-starved religious constituency to "The Beatles Are Here!" We too can fill our halls and draw our crowds!

But if success were the only peril which we had to withstand, the problem would not be too insurmountable. The issue thrusts down much deeper into that hidden dimension of life concerned with power. The handling of power is the inevitable consequence of exercising dominion. We have got it, and we have to use it. Power is the ability to accomplish purpose, and little can be done without the application of the appropriate degree of it at the right time. So here we are, called to proclaim the powerlessness of God from within the structures of power, and indeed, we need a power structure called the church in order to do it effectively. Surely he who does not recognize that there is in the most solemn of religious assemblies an element of power politics at work is not so much pious as naïve? In addition to those venerable categories of apostles, prophets, and martyrs, it is time the church paid liturgical tribute to its "holy jostle of power politicians" who, by their mastery of men, money, and machinery, accomplish much that is the kingdom in spite of the vilification of the religious proletariat.

Yet we know full well that power always exacts too high a price for its services. Ministers are peculiarly exposed to the temptations of power because they can claim, in a worldly sense, to have so little of it. It is easy to put a halo around the will to power we share with all men; to delude ourselves that because the end of all our activity is so laudable, this very fact purges and sanctifies the means we must use. We go with no apparent sense of incongruity from the endless sermon recitation of that dictum of Lord Acton's about power corrupting, etc., to the business of administering a church which is a multimillion-dollar empire with hundreds of thousands of employees, acres of property, vast overseas dependencies, as though the Holy Spirit rendered us miraculously immune from the touch of power's corrupting finger.

But we have no alternative. In order to be effective witnesses of the powerlessness of God, through which, regardless of the horror of the Jews and the sneers of the Gentiles, the ultimate thing is accomplished, we must touch, handle, and risk being destroyed by power.

This tension exacts its toil, and we might well envy those who cut the gordian knot and leave our company in order that they can responsibly exercise power and enjoy the legitimate fruits of it. For the rest of us, there is the haunting sight of a Richelieu, Wolsey, and Makarios, clutching their religious habits about them in the hope of protecting themselves from the spiritually deliberating effects of great power. It is not to be. We can neither enjoy power nor contract out of the use of it. From the village church council to the great denominational headquarters and through beyond to the ecumenical agencies, men of God must handle power and tremble at the enormity of their *hubris*.

3. *The Tensions of Knowledge*

One of the great fears of the contemporary minister is that of worldly irrelevance. He is acutely sensitive to the charge that he lives in a sheltered existence, insulated from the full pressures of the "real" world. In particular, he is faced with the challenge that he is the master of a body of knowledge which provides answers to questions that nobody is asking. His sense of insecurity is deepened by the constant invasion of secular disciplines into areas of human experience of which he was once sole interpreter. The social sciences, for example, have spawned a breed of secular priests whose insights into human personality and group behavior have dispossessed the minister of his freehold in the cure of souls.

It is the authority as well as the relevance of the body of sacred knowledge of which the minister is "professor" that is under question. Theology, the queen of sciences, is now jostled by all kinds of upstarts in the democracy of intellectual disciplines. She no longer has any *a priori* claim to be heard with respect. Her authority is solely that of the degree of receptivity she calls out in those who are open to her claims. The application of the scientific method to the biblical corpus has destroyed for all time the mystique once attached to it. The West has its *gurus* all right, but they are to be found in laboratories and not in pulpits.

These threats raise the question in acute form: What ought the minister to *know*? The paradox seems to be that the more extensive and profound his knowledge of the "sacred mysteries," the less able he is to communicate with the world to which these mysteries refer: the more he knows about his own subject, the less relevant he is judged by a world which has its own standards of knowledgeability. He is in a dilemma. In a world of specialisms, has he a corner on a certain discrete body of knowledge or must he range over the same ground as other specialists, sharing their presuppositions and having only the authority of competence in common disciplines?

The current cry is that in the church's dialogue with the world, the world must be allowed to write the agenda. The crucial issue is, however, whether besides asking the questions, the world is also the place where the answers are to be found. If this is so, then much of the minister's traditional knowledge appears to be irrelevant. He needs to acquire expertise in secular disciplines so that he will be able to hear and take part in this dialectual process of question and answer allegedly occurring in the world.

124

It cannot be gainsaid that a fundamentalism of either Bible or church which makes no attempt to come to terms with God's world except to use it as a captive audience does indeed render the modern minister irrelevant. But to go to the opposite extreme and proclaim the world's omnipotence in both asking and answering fundamental questions is to romanticize the secular disciplines. It is the assumption that in contrast to the church's uncertainty, the secular disciplines reveal a high degree of intelligibility where their understanding of values and ends is concerned. I do not think this is so. In their own way, the secular disciplines seem equally ambiguous in the answers they offer to key questions of our time.

It by no means follows that the minister who enters the contemporary debate on the basis of his mastery of a secular discipline rather than "sacred" knowledge will necessarily command an authority that his more clerically minded running mate has lost. He will be applauded for his versatility and rightly commended for trying to share the experience and tensions of the lay specialisms. But it is open to question whether his knowledge is any more "saving" knowledge than that of the biblical dogmatist.

Whatever claims are made for the world's right to ask the questions, it is surely a fact that the church addresses itself to them not in a spirit of empiricism but from the standpoint of biblical faith. The intelligent use of the Bible is the essential tool of the ministry. The world may not be interested in biblical answers to its questions, and that is sad, because these are the only ones the ministry is qualified to offer.

Though its relevance is a matter for argument, there is a body of knowledge of which the minister must be a master. And I suspect that many laymen are exasperated not because we cannot move with accustomed ease in their field, but by our failure to demonstrate that we are as much masters of our craft as they are of theirs. The blossoming of a generation of fairly competent sociologists, psychologists, and political theorists sporting clerical collars may indicate to the world that we take it seriously, but there is no reason to assume that ministers with much knowledge of theology and a fair knowledge of the social sciences are any more likely to hit the right targets than laymen with much knowledge of the social sciences and a fair knowledge of theology. Is not one cause of tension between laymen and ministry in the modern church the minister's insistence on trying to do the layman's job for him?

May I speak from personal experience? One of the great issues of the day in Africa is church-state relations. From one end of the continent to the other, churches are seeking a truly biblical stance toward governments which range from the *apartheid*-minded of South Africa to the restrictively Muslim of the Sudan. In my own attempts to lead the United Church of Zambia toward a sound relationship with the government of the newly independent Republic of Zambia, I cast about in all directions for guidance. Surprisingly, the clues I was seeking were furnished not by my textbooks on government and political theory, but by the writings of Karl Barth, of all people! It was the theologian of our day whose classical position has been one of lofty indifference to secular knowledge who has provided a massively biblical understanding of the role and limits of the state in his essay "The Community of Faith and the Secular Community" [1] which I found relevant and applicable to Zambia's situation.

Likewise, it has been to rather leaden commentaries on Old Testament books like Genesis and Exodus to which I have had to turn in order to gain understanding of the issues underlying the search for nationhood. Truly sensitive biblical interpretation can provide a standing ground detached from technical discussion and yet dominating it. For what strange arrogance is it that makes ministers assume that the expert will find their amateur critiques of complex

[1] Barth, *Against the Stream* (S.C.M. Press, 1954), pp. 15 ff.

issues of special value because those uttering them happen to be wearing clerical collars?

In the multiverse of the modern thought world, the minister cannot possibly be Renaissance man, equally competent in all fields of human knowledge. If his relevance depends upon mastery of the whole gamut of intellectual disciplines, then he *is* irrelevant and that is all there is to it.

Yet I do not believe that the mastery of biblical faith is an ivory-tower exercise remote from worldly involvement. Truly intelligent expositors of the Bible are gaining a hearing in our day. For it is often forgotten that they, too, are secular man. They are not immune from the pressures which are transforming the world. They are fully open to them. It is not a sequestered hermit who seeks a word from God, but a man of his time who is by virtue of secularizing forces that have either evolved from biblical faith or in reaction to it.

I would, however, stress that word "intelligent" exposition. The use of the Bible as an *Old Moore's Almanac* is to be deplored as bad craftsmanship and misuse of Scripture. Truly biblical exposition demands a high degree of critical intelligence and theological acumen. Above all, it calls for humility before the truth and the rejection of all claims to infallibility. I would make the claim that more ministers are robbed of relevance by their ignorance of what is in the Bible than by their ignorance of what is in the daily newspaper. Our task is to ensure that the word we speak on the events of the day is truly biblical rather than merely topical.

One other factor which bears upon the tensions of knowledge in the ministerial vocation must be mentioned. It relates to the existence of sacred as opposed to secular knowledge. A cliché of our time claims that Jesus, amongst other things, demolished forever the division between sacred and secular. If this is so, then there is only one comprehensive body of knowledge which minister and lay expert encounter on the same terms but at different points. There is, however, another viewpoint. The former Roman Catholic priest-theologian Mr. Charles Davis has swept away much of the confusion attaching to these ambiguous terms "sacred" and "secular." And his conclusion is that our new understanding of the meaning of the secular, far from abolishing the realm of the sacred, throws it into greater relief.

In his *God's Grace in History*, Mr. Davis writes:

> The sacred, then, is the area of mystery. Not mystery in the corrupted sense of an awkward puzzle, nor in the diminished sense of what yet awaits successful investigation. But mystery in the sense of a presence in man's experience of a darkness he knows to be a light but cannot see, of an intelligibility too bright for his gaze, of a transcendence that evokes his adoration. Mystery is the presence of God. Man cannot with truth locate that presence.[2]

God, therefore, is not a secular reality, nor ever could be. What he is in himself does not and never will come within human knowledge. But he does not choose to remain inaccessible. He has communicated himself. This is the burden of the gospel. If this is true, then there is a kind of knowledge which is totally outside the grasp of secular disciplines. It is, of course, equally inaccessible to theology as well. But it could be described as the awareness of a total ignorance. It is an intellectual agnosticism; a sensitivity to what can be known and what will never be knowable. This is essentially priestly knowledge. Of this the minister is truly guardian. Through worship and meditation and study, he approaches the fringes of that darkness which is light, but which man cannot see. Call me old-fashioned if you will, but I believe that the minister must, above all else, be a master of the knowledge of God's dealing with man's inner nature. He is the spiritual director of his people. In the old evangelical

[2] Davis, *God's Grace in History* (Fontana, 1966), p. 37.

parlance, he must know how to lead them to their Lord. This requires not only fervor and godliness but knowledge—not the knowledge that can be codified, but a body of truth all the same.

Certainly there are unresolvable tensions of knowledge in the ministerial vocation. No man can adequately cover both a wide area of secular discipline and sacred knowledge as well. How far he will cast the net of his inquiry will depend upon his background, temperament, experience, and training. The frontiers of the knowledge a minister feels called to master may be indistinct and vary from man to man, but the center is fixed. It is the saving knowledge of Jesus Christ.

4. *The Tensions of Security*

The paradox here is too obvious to need lengthy treatment. We are followers of One who "had not where to lay his head," called to live a debonair life of faith, responding gladly to the challenges of uncertainty; yet we are, alas, anchored like great blocks of concrete to certain conceptions of class and security. We must rate amongst the most secure members of the modern community—not the most affluent, and sometimes, possibly, the most embarrassed—but never the most vulnerable. There is much more chance of some of our members being thrown out of work or going bankrupt than there is of our failing to receive our modest salaries. And one thing we can take for granted. We shall always have somewhere to lay our heads—the house goes with the job.

By the same token, we who were meant to be "all things to all men"—outside the class structures in order to minister to all—are firmly planted alongside our professional colleagues in the law and medicine in the most prestigious sector of the middle class. Indeed, we have become a class image. We are fixed points of reference around which sociologists structure the middle class as they try to chart mobility from one class to another.

To some extent we are victims of a social revolution. The twentieth century has evolved a new understanding of family solidarity which places the welfare of children at the center of concern. We could hardly subject wives and children to the degree of insecurity that we personally might be prepared to accept in pursuit of our vocation. It is certainly true that in parts of the world where there is widespread violence and unrest, many missionaries have got to be withdrawn not because they are lacking in personal courage, but rather because of their fears for the safety of wives and children. And the greatest single cause of missionary resignation is the deterioration in educational standards in mission areas—an indication that in the modern world, missionaries will not sacrifice their children's future to their present tasks.

Those of us who work in Africa are conscious of the jarring contrast between our essential timidity and the utter abandon of orders such as White Fathers. Because they are celibate, they have no fears for their wives and children and so can move freely in troubled areas with easy consciences. Nor have they any private property, and so can symbolize Christ's identification with the poor because they are the only white men an African meets who have less than he has.

The reason the tensions of security are so acute is that the minister is suspended between the two extremes of utter sacrifice and the affluence of merit. Total sacrifice, of the kind where the source of the next meal is uncertain, is hard to face but is clear-cut, uncomplicated outworking of the gospel. Equally intelligible is the reward system based upon merit and qualification. The minister, however, is suspended in a limbo between the two. He is maintained to the level of what might be termed faded gentility. The sacrifices are there, all right, but are hidden, marginal, and debilitating.

This is a tension the ministry must live with. It causes twofold pangs of conscience, on the one hand that we are so secure in a world of chronic hunger, and on the other, that our children are denied some of the benefits of the good life by the sacrifices we do make in a meritocracy. This tension leads some men to part from our company, not because they are afraid of sacrifice, but they cannot live with ambiguity. It is also stimulating the search for patterns of ministry in which the source of income is secular employment. The weaknesses of the present structures are not the only cause of experiment. Some men leave us not because they are balked but because they are poor—yet their poverty does not seem to be of the kind which symbolizes anything of spiritual significance.

I have done. And having talked at length about ambiguities and tensions, I want to end with pointing to one aspect of ministry which is almost frighteningly unambiguous. In a very special sense, the minister is committed to the truth and vindication of the gospel by the simple fact that he is denied a whole range of secular satisfaction. Should the light of the gospel prove in the last day to have been darkness, the layman at least has the satisfaction of knowing that he has achieved some proximate goals, made some practical contribution to the life of the world. Not the ministry: we cannot point to having made a good chair, or passed a good parliamentary bill, or plowed a good field. All we have and are is vested in the truth of the gospel. And should the gospel not be true, then we are nothing, we have nothing, and we have done nothing. In sum: there is a degree of daring in the ministerial vocation which redeems any man's life from mediocrity. For we have committed ourselves to a vision. The justification of a whole lifetime and of many lifetimes rests upon a foundation as flimsy as a set of gospel promises.

If the gospel is true, we have everything. If it is false, we have nothing. And there is nothing ambiguous about that.

131

CHAPTER 12

The Rule of God over the
World of Nations: 1

Nothing infuriates the non-Christian more than the apparent inability of the Christians to speak a truly biblical word on national or international affairs which does not abound in paradox. Neither is the Christian allowed, apparently, to commit himself without reservation to any political position or ideology, nor grant more than churlish recognition to even the most laudable of the world's achievements.

It seems to men of goodwill, struggling manfully to realize mankind's great goals of a just social order and true world community, that whenever some progress has been made and a brick or two has been firmly planted, along will come the Christian, bearing in his hands a bucket of cold water, whose effect is to dissolve the cement and erase the ink on the blueprint. We are those who seem always to cry "Woe!" in the day of joy and who refuse to dance when others pipe. Yet is not the other half of our Lord's couplet also true—that we refuse to mourn when others weep and wail? When men's hearts fail them, their dreams dissolve and their world lies in ruins, behold the Christian with a cheery word of confidence in God's purposes for the very world about whose future prospects the same Christian was sadly shaking his head in more optimistic times! How justified is the world's irritation with us!

And yet the truth is surely not that we Christians are all spiritual Yorkshiremen, cantankerous by nature and happiest only when swimming against the stream. Our quixotic behavior is rooted much deeper in a biblical faith which will allow us to place little confidence in the institutions which the world has evolved to solve the problems of historical evidence—for we expect our salvation to come from outside. And if we appear remote and abstracted in the time of feverish plan-making, it is because none of the goals which might result from the working out of an ideology or philosophy within history has the slightest appeal for us—no utopia or Shangri-La, no proletariat revolution or Great Society.

Cynics are entitled to claim that we Christians want it both ways. We reserve the right to engage ourselves, on our own terms, in the political tasks of the moment, and should success follow, we ascribe the glory to God as a vindication of his providence. But when they fail, we wag the finger and say "We are not in the least bit surprised. That's just what the Bible told us to expect!" Maddening! In fact, of course, did the cynic but know it, far from any consciousness of having it both ways, it seems in our disillusioned moments that we get it neither way. We can see no vindication yet within history of the lordship of Christ upon whom all our hope is laid, and also we are denied the satisfaction of any earthly hope in the lasting value of the tasks we have to hand in the here and now.

We certainly don't choose to be such ill-humored traveling companions for our fellow pilgrims through history. What wouldn't we give for the Bible to sanction some political ideology so that we could throw ourselves into the task of shaping the world around it and die content in the knowledge that we have wrought something of lasting worth? If only we could share that secular optimism which sees man's progress as a golden arrow, cleanly cutting the air on its way to some target worthy of his stature and potentialities; instead of that tragic spiral as man, under the impetus of ever-increasing knowledge, soars higher and higher but always circles the same point, locked within the gravitational field of personal limitation he cannot break out of!

Instead, when we seek the Bible's word for our time, we find ourselves sitting down to a banquet of paradoxes garnished with dilemmas when we hoped for imperatives. How can a Christian evolve a political philosophy out of the contradictory and enigmatic material of the Bible? Unequivocal committal to the world, which is the essential condition of true political action, seems to be endorsed by the proclamation that God so loved the world that he gave his only Son that it might not be condemned but saved. But turn the page and we are confronted by a stern warning not to love the world and the assurance that friendship with the world will earn us God's undying enmity. How do you make practical politics out of that paradox? Or this. Our confidence in political institutions is bolstered by the assertion in Romans 13 that the state is of divine ordinance and then totally demolished in Revelation 13 by the flat statement that the state is the beast from Abyss. Where do we go from there? Or take the problems of the handling of power, central to every political issue, and apparently a legitimate Christian activity according to the biblical affirmation that we have been given "dominion." Behold, we are confronted with a Jesus who, according to Luke, endorses the handling of power by advising his disciples to buy swords, whilst Matthew trumpets at us that the same Jesus assured those who live by the sword that they would perish by it.

So massive and central are these biblical contradictions that only one of two explanations is possible. Either we must adopt the most mechanical view of the progressive revelation of God's truth in the Bible and assume that what is said chronologically later is to be preferred to what is said earlier as a clearer reflection of God's unfolding will, or else we face a possibility which is terrifying in its implications. It is that the Bible confronts us as a great slab of history with God's

134

footprints engraved upon it—a vast, untidy, messy picture of a world at whose heart are ambiguities so deep seated that it is impossible to address oneself to them except in paradox; that this is the world as it is and will continue to be through historical time—utterly resistant to all the attempts of the philosophers, priests, and kings to make sense of it; that trying to expose any ultimate meaning in history is like attempting to free your hands of a sticky flypaper—you release a finger only to entangle a thumb.

But if we take the Christian doctrine of redemption seriously, by what right could we expect any simpler, more rational explanation? If history had been a triumphant procession of cause and effect, transparent in meaning but swung slightly off course by the failure of men and nations to realize their destinies, then God's necessary action would have been limited to the letting loose of a redemptive idea which would have checked the drift and got the world back on track. Instead, the very rigorousness of God's action—the incarnation—indicates the centrality of ambiguity and the desperate difficulty in dealing with it within the limitations he has imposed upon himself. The total picture—the biblical picture—is of a universe rocked about its foundations, a cosmic upheaval, a widening circle of consequences, both good and bad, flowing from the demonic actions of men and societies. What political philosophy could make sense of that?

And if we are brutally frank, we must confess that at any given moment of time in the area of life with which we are dealing—mankind's collective relations—God's redemptive action and event, Jesus Christ, far from resolving the ambiguities of history, appears to deepen them. Well might we cast a longing, if fleeting, glance at a Marxism which sees the end of history from the beginning as a great monolithic structure within which even catastrophe is predictable and usable; where men need not wait for perfection to evolve from the working out of historical processes but can carry it

135

forward with them, justified in using any degree of guile or force against those who will not or cannot see what they see.

But it is not to be. No simple dogmatic assertions can really speak to the moral precariousness and ultimate tragedy of the whole human enterprise. The Christian is denied the luxury of being able to treat history as a series of problems and answers. Indeed, whenever we talk in terms of the "Christian" answer to a political problem, we have strayed far from biblical faith and are almost certainly reading into the situation our own ideological biases—as though hitting on the right course of action at the right time will clear a little ground from which we can begin the assault upon the next level of confusion until finally we arrive at some summit of icy clarity from which we shall see the pattern and meaning of all things spread out before us.

The Bible addresses the world in paradox in order to define the limits within which the divine and demonic operate in historical situations. It recognizes, with ruthless realism, that no human institution is likely to exist either in the pure form of an ordinance of God or as an utterly diabolic perversion of it, but will oscillate between these two poles. So the Christian finds himself speaking to the world a paradoxical word, the apparent contradictions of which serve both to encourage it in well-doing and act as a corrective to contemporary error and sinfulness. In other words, we speak not to offer a blueprint or lay down a policy so much as to respond to a mood.

What, then, is the contemporary mood of the world of nations to which biblical faith must speak and testify of God's rule? I would describe it as apocalyptic utopianism. The title of one of Peter Sellers' films put it much better and less pretentiously—*How I Learned to Love the Bomb and Stop Worrying!* Our postwar world has quickly learned to transmute its fears of atomic extinction into a strange hope. Because the unthinkable has not happened, hope grows of a world community flourishing in the shadow of the H-bomb's mushroom cloud, its unity assured by a balance of terror, its optimism vested in a gigantic paradox—the possibility of the instrument of our destruction becoming the guarantee of our security. Over the imposing entrances to our multiplying international institutions might be graven those words of Winston Churchill, "Peace shall be the study child of terror!"

Certainly there is little of the old liberal utopianism about. Two wars have purged the world of any expectation that universal brotherhood can issue from the conquest of the darker side of man's nature and the expression of his innate selflessness and goodwill. Ours is truly an apocalyptic utopianism because it is based upon the blinding perception that in the nuclear age the whole world is the smallest possible unit of survival. The appropriate image of our time is not the Greek one of man as Apollo, the charioteer of the sun, rising ever higher, untramelled in achievement, but an African one of man welded into one tribe by the fear of a common enemy, huddled round the fire, friend and foe alike, driven together by terror of the nameless things in the dark beyond the flickering light.

Yet there is impressive evidence that the world has succeeded in making law out of its necessity. The dogged survival, against all odds, of the United Nations Organization; the international agencies which testify to the fact that there are certain elemental things such as food and education and health which the whole world owes to any part of it; the evolution of a sketchy international morality, whose existence nations acknowledge, even in their breach of it, by their attempts at self-justification—all these symbolize the struggle for world community. Thanks be to Hiroshima and Nagasaki for their wonderful gift—fear more potent than love and more durable than goodwill!

This strange hope is also bolstered by another great reality of our time which is partly a by-product of the balance of power which the nuclear age has made inevitable—the collapse of the old empires and the rapid spread of nation-hood. Willingly or unwillingly, the right of peoples to become nations has been conceded and has found expression in the appearance of hundreds of new sovereign states, many with unpronounceable names, all desirous of expressing their peculiar genius through political institutions they have created, borrowed, or inherited. Rich new content has been poured into the concept of the nation as men of many races for the first time savor the strange pride of patriotism and the rich, heady wine of selfhood. And the technology which has made one world a scientific miracle has been harnessed to guarantee the viability of these new nations, spawning highways, bridges, universities, dams, modern cities, industrial complexes where once was desert, jungle, silence, darkness. It is as though some giant hand has scooped up the amorphous sands of mankind and molded them into the hard national bricks from which the structure of world community can be built.

So men have emerged from their deep shelters and are making yet another attempt to build a tower up to heaven, which this time, thanks to modern communications, need be no Babel. And in many areas of the world, the church has been caught up in this intoxication. For the first time since the end of the liberal era, it is possible to hear Christian prophets talking about a historical kingdom of God as a biblical skeleton, fleshed out into the shape of existing or hoped-for international institutions. In the most unlikely quarters, men are succumbing to the old Marxist heresy that history has a political goal, and ignored is the somber biblical truth that the meaning of history is found only beyond itself; that the new heaven and earth are not the final shapes wrought out of the material of history, but are the gifts of God from beyond.

Upon this scene of frenetic activity, the Christian bursts

138

with a word which sounds as appropriate as the choir singing "Sheep may safely graze" at the butcher's funeral. It is the paradoxical word which God speaks, according to Genesis, as he surveys the original Tower of Babel—"You have done well. Therefore I will bring your efforts to nought!" A word which sounds to the world and possibly the Christian charged to deliver it both monstrously unjust and utterly opaque—a word which combines both blessing and curse; a riddle, a lifting of one hand in benediction whilst the other fist crashes down in anathema.

God's word to the nations is one of blessing for every effort of mankind to win a little more order from chaos; for every political arrangement within which men can be more truly human; for every evidence of responsible stewardship of God-given resources; for every sign of national transcendence in the willingness of powerful nations to allow the moral claims of the weaker against the stronger; for painstaking negotiation and cool-nerved statesmanship which have enabled the world to skirt the brink of disaster.

You have done well, says God. Therefore I will bring your efforts to nought. Why? cries the politician, the humanitarian, the man of goodwill. In God's name, Why? Can we do better than our best? We are men, not gods!

The teaching of Jesus spells the death of apocalyptic or any other utopianism, for it demonstrates that we have put our trust in that which cannot save when we expect unalloyed good to issue from any human institution, and especially those institutions which constitute the highest degree of man's togetherness—the nation and the world of nations. Ill-received though it might be, we are required to administer a large dose of biblical deflation to man's trust in the power, authority, and status of the nation. We must expose it as theologically defective, morally blind, and transient, and therefore unable to bear the weight of all the hope men have placed upon it.

When we hear it claimed for a nation that it is enlightened, responsible, and generous, we are forced to retort with Paul, "Your nation is separated from Christ, alienated from the Commonwealth of Israel, a stranger to the covenant of promise, having no hope and without God in the world!" (Eph. 2:12). When national leaders and statesmen are prone to pride themselves on their realism, percipience, and clear-sightedness, we must echo Paul's flat statement—the nations are blind—to God, to themselves and to all men (Rom. 1:24, 29).

These rigorous, pessimistic biblical judgments upon the nation must be clearly sounded because, as Reinhold Niebuhr has eloquently demonstrated in his epoch-making *Moral Man and Immoral Society*, the nation, by virtue of the fact that it embodies the largest concentration of earthly power, is prone to a monstrous egotism and idolatry, claiming universality for its values and seeking a pseudo-immortality.

Because it is the contemporary mood for nations to pride themselves on their scientific achievements, their enlightened laws, their foreign aid appropriations—to measure themselves approvingly against their rivals—it is necessary to point out that God shows a massive indifference toward national achievement. At the level at which his judgment operates, the distinction between righteous and unrighteous nations is obscured, and a coming to terms with this truth is the only possible source of humility in nations which are tempted to regard their good fortune as proof of their virtue.

So our tendency to assume that our democratic system is of God and that of the communists is of the Devil is a blasphemy, and any belief that our nation is closer to the kingdom of God than theirs is a delusion. Democrats and totalitarians, advanced and underdeveloped nations, civilized and backward societies are all unceremoniously lumped together by God and constitute that "mere drop in the bucket" of which Isaiah speaks. China with her 600 million people, the U.S.A.

140

with her trillions of dollars, Britain with her thousand years of democracy all share "the gross darkness that covers the peoples" with those nations they regard as enemies of their national survival and threats to world peace.

Indeed, I find myself more and more reluctant to think in terms of God having a special will for the particular nation as opposed to the nations. That evocative juxtaposition of Bible and national flag central to civic ceremonial seems to me productive of an identification of national policy with the divine will which reinforces that monstrous egotism of which Niebuhr has written. Quite apart from the ever-present danger of fascism, there seems to be little biblical ground for the assumption that God finds any value in our national particularities or desires to use those elements of nationality which mark us off from other peoples to further his purposes. It must surely have been in one of those rare moments when Victorian fervor overwhelmed profound biblical insight that the great F. D. Maurice declaimed, "We cannot attain Christ's likeness if we do not care for England as he cared for Palestine. We have as much right to call England a Holy Nation as the prophets had to call Judea a Holy Nation!" It is truly ironic that Maurice's proclamation of England and the Holy Nation should coincide with the opening of the intensive phase of her imperialist policy, the consequences of which, in Asia and Africa, have demonstrated that inextricable mixture of good and evil of which Jesus talked, and have revealed how morally ambiguous are the actions of even the most civilized of nations.

There is one exception to this stricture on placing too much weight upon the idea of God's will for the nation as opposed to the world of nations. We have New Testament warrant for distinguishing one nation from the nations in the sense that its peculiar identity is part of God's purpose, and its separateness a testimony to the world. That Holy Nation is not, alas, Great Britain, but the New Israel, whose citizens are drawn from every nation under heaven, and which is marked off from the world of nations in several important ways. Her citizens, unlike those of the nations, are called and chosen rather than thrown together by biological accident. The Christ who is hidden within the nations is manifest in and reigns over the New Israel. Where the nations are agglomerations of great power and maintain themselves by the exercise of it, the New Israel glories in her powerlessness, choosing suffering rather than self-assertion as her key signature. And the conflicts of color, class, and special interest groups which are resolved by compromise within the nations are totally transcended in the New Israel by reconciliation, the destruction of all particularities through and in Jesus Christ.

It might well be legitimately charged that the endorsement of this harsh biblical view of the status of the nations robs the Christian of any ground from which he can speak or act in a politically relevant manner, for we seem to have written off the entire problem assumed in the title by consigning the world of nations to an outer darkness beyond hope and lost from God. In fact, it would be my claim that truly relevant political action as testimony to God's rule over the world of nations can only issue from the abandonment of any secular hope for them. And that the clear distinction drawn between God's will for the Nation—the New Israel—and the nations provides the essential base from which this testimony can be offered.

CHAPTER 13

The Rule of God over the World of Nations: 2

How, then, does the New Israel testify to the rule of God over the world of nations? It has a threefold mode of operation—the evangelical, the prophetic, and the eschatological—each one of which takes the ambiguity of history seriously; the first in the human heart, the second in the sphere of immediate political activity, and the third in the total meaning of history. And it must be emphasized that at each of these three levels of action, the citizens of the New Israel are forced to wrestle with paradox.

THE EVANGELICAL DIMENSION OF THE LIFE OF THE NEW ISRAEL

It is clear that from the earliest times the church has never been allowed to regard the plight of the nations with either contempt or complacency, for they have treasure to bring into the New Jerusalem. She has lived always under a powerful missionary compulsion to preach the gospel to all nations so that, against Christ's return, there should be found in every land the first fruits of the harvest he will accomplish. The New Israel exists as a mission to and in the nation within which it is set, testifying to God's claim upon it and presenting a living picture of what redemption could mean to its life—for this New Israel is made of the same material as the world, but it is the world shot through with the redemptive power of God. Within the nation, the New Israel testifies to God's rule by proclamation of Christ's lordship, by the office of intercession, and by a quality of witness which is a steadfast refusal to allow the commands of God to take second place to those of men; a witness which reminds the nation that its primary engagement is with God.

The evangelical imperative serves, too, to offer the nation proof that God graciously acts within history. This proof is a matter not of philosophical speculation but of personal encounter—the humility, true repentance, creativity, and lack of pride which are characteristics of those who have been with Jesus.

Unless the gospel offer occupies the forefront of the life of the New Israel, the other dimensions of her activity are bound to degenerate into a vapid moralizing, eloquently described by Richard Niebuhr's epigram as testifying to a "God without wrath, who brings men without sin into a kingdom without judgment through a Christ without a Cross!" It must never be forgotten that the first outpost of God's rule over the nations is the human heart; that whatever may be the social and political implications of Jesus' teaching, he is first and foremost concerned with the quality of the personal life of his subjects. Though all the ills of the body politic cannot be ascribed to human sinfulness, many can, and therefore this personal source of evil intent must be radically dealt with.

But the evangelical concern of the New Israel must not be interpreted narrowly as spiritualizing men out of concrete human situations. It is not merely the person within the nation who needs to be redeemed, but also those elements of nationality which divide him from other men, within which he hides and which are expressions of his egotism and self-assertiveness. The frontiers crossed by the gospel are not only those on the maps but also those in the human mind. Truly evangelical proclamation always strikes at a pressure point in conduct; it is never confined to the welfare of the soul in the abstract. The validity of our conversion is attested by the power to deal with our most persistent and character-istic social sins. I would challenge the adequacy of any gospel proclamation which allowed a man to come to Christ in South Africa or the southern states of the U.S. but left his racial attitudes unchanged; or did not affect tribal prejudices in Africa; or jingoism in China; materialism in the West; xenophobia in Asia, and so on. Though it is always dangerous to talk about national sins, since the detection of them is more often symptomatic of the observer's envy than anything else, nevertheless our history, tradition, experiences, characteristic power structure do predispose us to certain moral weaknesses of nationality which need to be redeemed. In this sense, it is part of the evangelical role of the New Israel to elevate the mind and purify the heart of the nation. And that is a politically relevant contribution.

But here we must grapple with a paradox which cannot be evaded in considering the evangelical dimension of the New Israel's testimony to God's rule over the nations. I would express it as follows. The particular fruit of the evangelical experience which Christians seek conscientiously to apply in the fields of political and international affairs is the love ethic. And there is no doubt that Jesus enjoined the law of love upon his followers—whatever else in the Gospels is obscure, that most certainly is not. Yet the paradox is this. The love ethic we are commanded to make the law of our being is, by definition, impossible of fulfillment within history. And further, if we attempt to carry it through too rigorously, we forfeit any possibility of relevant political judgment and action, and indeed, pressed to its limit, it becomes self-defeating and destructive.

It could, of course, be retorted that the paradox I am stating is a false one; that the love ethic only seems impossible of fulfillment because no group or nation has yet had the courage to test it. And no doubt you could also quote G. K. Chesterton's aphorism that it is not that Christianity has

145

been tried and found wanting, but that it has been found hard and not tried. But I would maintain that this paradox is a genuine one in the sense that the Bible itself furnishes proof of it. The heart of biblical truth—the cross—is at one and the same time the utter vindication of the love ethic and also positive proof that this ethic is beyond fulfillment within history and certainly in the area of political action.

The classical theory of the atonement depicts a struggle between the crucified Christ and the legions of hell which is cosmic in its significance. Though defeated in principle, these powers in fact still operate to extend the area of chaos not solely in the human heart and in the realm of interpersonal relations, but also within the collective institutions of society. It is all too clear that in concrete historical situations the only barrier against the onset of this chaos is the use of a degree of constructive power, involving compulsion, which the pure love ethic must rule out of court. Indeed, it is good Reformation theology that the state as sword-bearer has its origins in the fall of man, where the breakup of the original pattern of divine order resulted in the necessity of a degree of compulsion to impose order and social cohesion upon the life of man.

Or if you expose the moral meaning of the cross at its simplest, which demonstrates the truth that love can only be fully realized at the expense of life itself, it is obvious that whereas an individual can choose the way of the cross, no larger grouping such as a nation ever has or ever will. For according to the love ethic, the way of sacrifice must be personally and freely chosen; no one can either enjoin it upon others or choose it for them without destroying the basis of the ethic. One could go further and claim that if any degree of validity is accorded to the state as a divine ordinance, it exists for purposes which are the precise opposite of the way of love unto death. It is the purpose of the state to preserve life, to shield its members from extinction whether threatened

146

by outside enemy, internal chaos, or natural hazard. That is what the state is for, and therefore it has a divine function which, within the ambiguities of history, is the precise contrary of the ultimate logic of the love ethic—fulfillment at the expense of life itself. So the attempt to enjoin the love ethic upon the state is to invite it to deny the law of its being.

The truth is that the love ethic in its pure form cannot come to terms with the compulsion which is a necessary feature of all organized life. And it obscures political problems when it causes Christians to seek an ideal possibility in situations which offer only a number of realistic alternatives, none ideal, few satisfactory, all morally relative. Follow the love ethic through to its limit, and it will deny the Christian any participation in political life at all because he will seek in vain for a political system pure enough to deserve his devotion.

Unless the Christian is to retire to the mountaintop and pray his life away, he must operate within society as a responsible man, which means that in certain fields he must make decisions on behalf of others—in industry, through the ballot box, within the family circle. He is perfectly entitled to follow the love ethic in sacrificing his own interests without hope of reward, but he cannot justify the sacrifice of interests other than his own. He cannot compel those for whom he is responsible to choose sacrifice. Hence, willingly or unwillingly, he must follow the hard law of collective relations and choose the only kind of justice that society has ever known—that which issues from the harmonizing of legitimate conflicts of interests, if necessary by the imposition of superior power. And when he has got that far, he is thinking politically. He has faced up to the unpalatable fact that all collective relations are so morally obtuse as to make a strategy of pure disinterestedness impossible.

The unwillingness to accept the tensions which this paradox sets up results in the prevalent political heresy of evangelical Christianity. It is the belief that if only men would love one another, all political problems would disappear, since the necessity for politics at all stems from a selfishness which men could easily transcend if they had the will. Its stablemate in the realm of international affairs is the assumption that the fervent preaching of the gospel, leading to the conversion of sufficient citizens of sufficient countries, will bring to pass a Christian world government. So will the Christmas angel's prophecy be fulfilled—peace on earth will result from the actions of men of goodwill.

The fallacy of this majestically simple theological position can easily be exposed by examining the life of the Christian church, whose members, by definition, are committed to the law of love and are, or ought to be, converted men, yet within which conflicts of interest, problems of power and authority occur which must often be settled (dare one say it?) by political means. How much more the state and the world of nations who make for themselves no impressive claims to a knowledge of divine truth or the power to live it out in community?

Most serious of all, this lofty indifference to the complexity of political problems and the insistence on attributing all national and international tensions to simple unbelief lead to monstrous paradies of the true evangelical role of the New Israel. It enables the most effective mass evangelist of our time to wash his hands, in a public statement, of the Vietnam tragedy as the responsibility of the politician because his job is to preach the gospel. It provides thousands of Christians, all devout and sincere, with justification for blinding themselves to the stark injustices of racial discrimination in their land, city, or street because their business is to offer all men Christ, but only some of them a seat in their parlor or a vote in their elections.

It provided many missionaries in Africa and Asia with a pseudo-biblical warrant for resisting the claims of subject peoples for freedom and self-determination, marking off the New Israel from the political arena so absolutely that young nationalist Christians were forced to make a straight choice—their political allegiance or their church membership.

Is it possible to take to ourselves the tensions involved in both attempting to obey the law of love and yet recognizing the impossibility of its fulfillment within history? Certainly there is no way forward in striking such a paradox asunder and cleaving to the half which it is least painful to come to terms with. Neither in a personal pietism which is too naïve to recognize that in refusing to make political decisions one is making a political decision with terrifying implications, nor in a worldly cynicism which abandons altogether the attempt to make relevant the impossible law of love and accepts the power structures of this world on their own terms, is there any possibility of achieving that truly biblical stance which describes the New Israel as being in the world but not of it.

THE PROPHETIC DIMENSION OF THE LIFE OF THE NEW ISRAEL

The very possibility of prophetic action by the New Israel depends upon a paradox. The only way we can act prophetically within the world of nations is to grant them a status which, in our evangelical role, we must categorically deny. In evangelism we must offer Christ to a lost world, to warn men to "flee from the wrath to come." In prophecy we are seeking to encounter what Niebuhr calls the "Hidden Christ" within history; to search him out where he is doing some good thing in an area beyond hope. Obviously, therefore, however pessimistic may be the ultimate theological judgment upon the nations, there are still in the here and now proximate goals, various levels of achievement, morally significant situations which demand a response from us.

Here, of course, is the point at which our abandonment of

any hope for the nations allows us a freedom to operate within specific political situations, to accept the immediate task as worthy of our very best efforts. For the great danger of all political action is that it tends to absolutize itself—to project itself forward into the future toward some great historical denouement. Every political ideology incorporates its own eschatology—a doctrine of "last things" in terms of which the past and the present are given a meaning. It is of the nature of truth in the political realm that if it is carried through too consistently, it becomes falsehood. (It is the great merit of democracy that it rarely allows any political ideology to be worked out to its logical conclusion without modifying it by the flux of public opinion through the ballot box.) The Christian is able to bear his share of responsibility for the good order and justice of the community, free to seek the truth of the moment, accepting the limits of the possible. He need fall prey to no political messiah, inerrant ideological word, inner voice of fanaticism—all inviting him to leap from the pinnacle of the temple in order to inherit the kingdoms of this world.

The most important of all the prophetic gifts of the New Israel is political realism—a freedom both from utopian optimism and fanatical despair. We above all men recognize that the effectiveness of politics lies in its harnessing to constructive purposes morally dangerous forces. The self-regard and national pride, which Christians are required to shun like the Devil, are the forces which the politician must use to motivate men for socially beneficial ends. Listen to a debate in the House of Commons or the Senate of the United States on aid to underdeveloped countries. The moralist delivers a fervent oration on the reality of the one-world family and the responsibility of the well endowed for the weak and poor. But it is the politican who gets the bill through by pointing out that communism feeds upon poverty, and that if we do not do something for Africa and Asia, the

150

Chinese will. So the end result is an act of political morality, achieved by the beguiling of deadly dangerous sentiments.

To condemn this hard truth about political motivation as evidence that politics is "a dirty game" is a pious hypocrisy, and to pretend that there is some other more enlightened, noble means of accomplishing political ends is a delusion. You might charge that this is a very cynical view of politics, yet surely the God who maketh the wrath of men to praise him can also use their prudent self-interest to induce them to accept larger claims and wider responsibilities. The ambiguities of political morality cannot be evaded. The suggestion that in politics, the Christian alone can march confidently forward through the murk, guided by heavenly radar, speaking what is true and doing what is good whilst others wallow in confusion and compromise, is a piece of gratuitous nonsense which will survive neither the realism of the Bible nor the experience of history. The Christian politician is not wrong less often than others—though he may tend to be wrong about different things. All politicians are limited by the material they must use. The sculptor may have a soul as pure as driven snow, but he must still get his hands dirty if he wishes to model in clay. If we wish to speak and act in political terms, we are forced to deal in power in order to get a rough approximation of justice in any area where interests clash. And the truth about power is that it always exacts too high a price for its services. We may proclaim the theological truth that it is utterly futile to attempt to organize life around the self—personal or collective—yet we shall discover that often and again the dynamic energy released by this egotism is the only force available to motivate men toward good ends.

Thus, it is part of the prophetic role of the New Israel to free Christians from illusions about what is possible and not possible in politics—to get those who are committed to the Great Absolute—God—to see value in the relative—tentative harmonies, provisional equalities, proximate

151

justice—for nothing grander, more sublime is likely to emerge from political action within history.

But to heap paradox upon paradox, the New Israel as prophet must sacrifice a degree of relevance in order to be truly relevant to the life of the world of nations. Take, for example, the question of justice. The Bible's view of justice, as thundered forth by the prophets, is nothing like so simple, sublime, and cogent as Aristotle's majestic "To each his due!" The prophets would have none of this business of equal justice. They declaimed that God was angry with princes and kings because they turned the poor away from their doors. Biblical justice always has a built-in bias toward the little people of the earth—"He has torn imperial powers from their thrones, but the humble have been lifted high. The hungry he has satisfied with good things, the rich sent empty away." The Bible is certainly not a politically impartial book. It announces that God is against all concentrations of power and wealth and influence, however legitimately obtained and benevolently used.

Or take the power of imagination through which God enables the Christian to identify himself with others, "put himself in their shoes," sense how they are feeling. The political value of this gift is beyond question, for it enables us to penetrate the barriers of perception and get some idea of what our policy looks like from the other side of the Iron Curtain or east of Suez or south of the Equator or on the wrong side of the breadline or from the Negro side of the town.

Or consider the highest exercise of earthly love—the love of one's enemies and the forgiveness of wrongdoers. Without doubt there are socially redemptive possibilities, in the strictest political sense, from the discriminating exercise of this degree of forbearance, not to mention the embarrassment we would be saved whenever we have got to stop punishing former enemy nations in order to build them up militarily so that they can form part of our defense bloc against our former ally, the new enemy.

Now none of these political qualities, to which the New Israel testifies, is relevant in the sense that it is an accepted value of politics, a logical outworking of any forces operating within the concrete situation. Yet each of these qualities is supremely relevant because it testifies to the truth that the nation's main engagement is with God, not with an economic crisis, a strategic problem, a political dilemma. We are required to sacrifice relevance in the sense of speaking solely in terms of what is given in order to be relevant in the sense of identifying the true seat of ambiguity and exposing it before God.

THE ESCHATOLOGICAL DIMENSION OF THE LIFE OF THE NEW ISRAEL

"Till he come. . . ." This challenging phrase leads us straight to the heart of the eschatological dimension of the action of the New Israel in testifying to God's rule over the world of nations. The paradox is easily stated but virtually impossible to discuss. The New Israel is called to live out its life in the midst of the world of nations as though something utterly beyond human comprehension had actually occurred; to testify to that which cannot be put into words—to point the nations to an utterly-beyond-history in the midst of history.

How does this whole business of the human enterprise end? What form will the grand finale of the glorious, tragic pageant of history take? Anyone who can rise above his own immediate interests and project himself beyond his own life-span must wrestle with this question. And if he is reasonably intelligent, he will be seeking not so much an answer as a reassurance. He will not delude himself that this great sprawling thing we call history can be summarized in a simple, intelligible statement—an original, luminous truth. But he does want to know that the end result is not an end

153

without an end, utter futility, aimlessness, as though humanity were adrift on some raft in a limitless ocean, carried now
this way and that, but never getting any closer to land. He
would like to feel that all that has been nobly and well
wrought by mankind will not be as evanescent as the sculpting
of elaborate shapes in the sand, destined to be washed away
by the next tide.

Whether the Bible's answer to his heart-cry will nourish
hope or despair depends upon his faith. Certainly we are not
permitted to treat history like some detective story, where in
the last chapter and the last paragraph the significance of the
obscure becomes plain, every enigmatic word and gesture
and action falls into a pattern we ought to have been able to
trace all the way through, had we been clever enough. The
last page, paragraph, and sentence of history will be a record
of the same old order and chaos, ambiguity and meaning,
good and evil.

For biblical faith, the meaning of history is seen as being
beyond itself. We are not waiting for something to happen *in*
history, but for something to happen *to* history. We can grasp
this much; that for mankind the kingdom whose seed is
hidden within history will be perfected, and history must end
before it is fully revealed, even as the seed of eternal life in the
heart of the individual believer needs death to make it
manifest. And we know that Christ will do this thing; that
what he has accomplished through the total redemptive event
will become fully plain. His return in clouds of glory is a
metaphor of the bringing of transparent clarity to all the
affairs of men and nations, the tearing away of all veils, the
restoration of everything that has been destroyed—the gift of
a new heaven and earth which will render both church and
state null and void, for the New Jerusalem has neither
temple nor sword.

Now since by definition what happens beyond history can
be neither described nor comprehended, we could well

154

pigeonhole the whole area of Christian eschatology, claiming
that it is pointless, our worrying about what we cannot be
expected to understand. But it is not to be. The New Israel is
commanded to live with the end as a present reality rather
than a tentative hope. It is made clear to us that the end is
not what comes *after* everything else but what has been
inaugurated by the Christ-event, and since we cannot
possibly claim ignorance of the fact that the Christ-event *has*
taken place, we must also take seriously the implications of
Christian eschatology for our life and conduct.

The apparent contradictions in the New Testament
between the kingdom of God as a present reality and as an
imminent event do not trouble us too much as an intellectual
problem, for having swallowed the camel of the presence of
the end from beyond history, we do not have too much
difficulty in digesting the gnat of the weird concept of time
this must involve. So we can face up manfully to paradoxes
such as Christ saying both "The kingdom is come upon
you. . ." and "Pray . . . thy kingdom come on earth. . . ." But
the question which is more daunting is this. What are the
political implications of eschatology? What is the significance
for the world of nations of the presence within history of the
utterly-beyond-history?

Albert Schweitzer once wrote an influential book whose
title could be translated into English *The Secret of the
Kingly Rule of God*. It speaks of the Jesus who, whenever he
had performed one of the miracles which were signs of the
kingdom, warned those who had eyes to understand the
significance of what had happened that they should "tell no
man!" The kingly rule of God over the nations is a secret. It
is not to be spoken of lightly nor can its relationship to
specific political and international events be announced with
any degree of confidence. Why? Because the open proclamation of it to those who cannot understand will do little more
than add one more area of ambiguity to already confused

situations. Indeed, to designate a concrete historical happening as an outworking of God's will is to subject him to the relativities of good and evil within time.

The wisdom of this diffidence is reinforced by the nature of political truth itself. It is characteristic of political decisions that they can rarely be described in principle as right or wrong. They are only proved to be right or wrong by their consequences. Should Britain enter the Common Market? Even after a full and careful analysis of all the facts has been made, no answer in principle is possible. The decision to enter or stay out of the Common Market will only be revealed to have been right or wrong in the light of its consequences. Hence, the "crunch" of a political decision may only come in five or ten or twenty years' time. What did Jesus say? "God's wisdom is proved right by its results" (Matt. 19:11). Confident declarations in principle that God's will is embodied in a political policy or the general stance of the nation in an international crisis are less likely to be prophetic than foolhardy. The kingly rule of God is a secret because we must not "use" him—enlist him to our schemes, seek his sanction for policies which are shot through with our national self-assertiveness and, therefore, doomed. God's will is both so simple that a single fallible human being can respond to it, and yet so majestic that it bursts out of any attempt to contain it within a national policy or an international situation.

Certainly a prophet called Isaiah could put into the mouth of God the words "Ho, Assyria, the rod of my anger and the staff of my fury!" But in the modern world, judgments of this order are more likely to issue from our partisanship and subtle political analysis than from any confidence of speaking a divine truth. Ask a group of Christians from two contending nations to interpret into modern dress a slice of Bible history like this passage from Isaiah, and it will be too clear that Assyria is the nation that oppresses us, resists our will, challenges our supremacy. We will go so far as to grant it the status of a scourge in God's hands, but we are in no doubt who represents Israel. We do!

So though the New Israel is ever conscious of God's rule over the nations, she is reverently agnostic about the concrete political events which are revealed as bearers of it. The world may cry "Thank God!" when some miraculous deliverance is received or curse God when a disaster occurs, in no doubt that the extraordinary is God's doing, but the New Israel keeps her secret well. She is too conscious of the imminence of the end to attempt to usurp the role of her Lord as judge of all the earth. His finger, and his alone, points to what will be established and what cast down; what in history has borne God's will and what has been smashed by it.

Only in one way can the New Israel be sure that her proclamation of God's kingly rule is not in error and that is when, by the power of Christ, she performs those miracles which are the signs of the kingdom—and they can rarely be translated into the material of political policies with any close degree of relevance.

It might be thought that this attitude of agnosticism about the concrete evidence of God's rule must restrict the church to an otherworldly pietism, dumb and paralyzed before the events of our time. But it is the very fact that God's kingly rule is a secret within the world that lends moral urgency to our actions in the political realm. For if we could proclaim with utter confidence that God's will demanded this or that course of action, then the result would be complacency and arrogance, a nonchalant reliance upon God to vindicate his own plans. Instead, we are those who must see every political issue as demanding knife-edge moral application and prophetic insight lest, when all things are made plain, we are revealed as having confused the trivial and the important, and discarded as of no great significance the fulcrum about which God was to move the nations. Because the world is prone to make facile distinctions between what are called major and minor political issues, the seeds of catastrophe and war often drop unnoticed in some obscure corner and germinate in darkness until they burst forth in a poisonous growth that desolates the earth. The Christian who is vigilant to enter into the mystery of the kingdom and seek out the evidence of God's rule ought to be the one least likely to overlook the tiny hinges upon which great things move. Put in political terms, his gifts to the dialogue of our time ought to be subtlety, sensitivity, and keen moral perception, for his search for the secret will make a politician out of him.

That word "vigilance" reminds me of another aspect of the eschatological dimension of the action of the New Israel. It is right that we should thrill to the rich imagery of the return of our Lord in the vision captured in verse by Charles Wesley:

> Lo, he comes with clouds descending,
> Once for ransomed sinners slain,
> Thousand, thousand saints attending
> Swell the triumph of his train!

But we must not be so carried away by it all that we fall into the trap of assuming that this explosive bursting into history of God's reality will be the first inkling we shall have that the consummation of history is upon us. Nor should we be so seduced by that phrase "the second coming of our Lord" that we imagine that in the meantime he is somewhere else, in heaven perhaps, preparing for his triumphal entry into history for the second and last time. There are New Testament images which describe our Lord sneaking back into history like a burglar at night or like the unannounced return of our boss when we thought he was safely away on holiday. In other words, it is a biblical insight that the One who will come again is always coming, imperceptibly, silently, persistently. How the concept of his constant entering into specific historical situations can be reconciled with the vision of a final consummation, I really wouldn't know unless it is to be seen as a problem of the inability of spatial language to describe what is both timeless and timely. However, the problem is not the concept but the reality—Christ confronting us as the end in the midst of history in imperceptible ways. But how?

Well, if the personality of Christ the Judge bears any relationship to that of the historical Jesus, we can be sure that the One who is always coming encounters us in the form of the casualties of this world, the lonely, broken, outcast, imprisoned, defeated, dying. He slips into history and confronts us with the end in shape of those right under our noses who are easiest ignored, or whose plight is too painful or costly for us to ameliorate.

Translate this eschatological truth into political terms, and it means that the members of the New Israel engage in the battle against poverty, disease, racial discrimination, injustice, and oppression, not as a humanitarian concern, but as an acknowledgment of the presence of the One who always comes in a hungry child, a despised man of another skin pigmentation, an oppressed minority. And the judgment upon us if we should be careless and complacent is correspondingly severe. It is a theological judgment, not merely a failure of human concern or lack of benevolence. We have been found wanting at the end. The New Israel as watchman has failed in vigilance and not noticed that the thief in the night has slipped past us as we strutted proudly in our lofty perches. Charles Peguy once said that everything begins in mysticism and ends in politics. Certainly the mystical vision of our Lord's glorious return ought to be the inspiration of a political radicalism which makes most current expressions of political radicalism seem pallidly conservative. We can never ever be sure whether the next person we meet on the street, color, race, and class apart, who has a claim upon us, confronts us as a casual encounter or an ultimate judgment.

Christian eschatology presents us with the vision of a world of nations haunted by the presence of the one who is the object of all national policies and political programs—the Son of Man—man who is the goal of history, not man as he is, but whose true being is revealed in Christ.

Now I have finished, except to add one final word. The greatest proof of God's rule over the world of nations consists not in any of the dimensions of the action of the New Israel I have described, but in her very survival. Against all odds, assaulted from without and sapped from within, lifted up and cast down, never permitted to rest but always on the move, the story of the New Israel has been one of sudden ends and strange new beginnings, of decay and restoration, of death and resurrection, of humiliation and glory. To what end? To the end simply that in every time and place, in a thousand accents, she can cry in the midst of the world of nations, "Fear God and give him glory, ye who dwell upon the face of the earth, of every nation and tribe and tongue and people, for the hour of judgment has come."